Winning Ways

Achieving Zero-Defect Service

Winning Ways
Achieving Zero-Defect Service

Jacques Horovitz
Foreword by Gilbert Trigano

Productivity Press

CAMBRIDGE, MASSACHUSETTS

NORWALK, CONNECTICUT

Productivity Press
P.O. Box 3007
Cambridge, Massachusetts 02140
(617) 497-5146 (telephone)
(617) 868-3524 (telefax)

Cover design by Micki Amick
Typeset by Rudra Press, Cambridge, Massachusetts
Printed and bound by Maple-Vail Book Manufacuturing Group
Printed in the United States of America
Printed on acid-free paper

Library of Congress Cataloging-in-Publication Data

Horovitz, Jacques, 1947-
  [Qualité de service. English]
  Quality customer service: winning ways/Jacques Horovitz:
preface by Gilbeft Trigano
    p.   cm.

  Translation of: La qualité de service.
  Includes bibliographical references.
  ISBN 0-915299-78-X (alk. paper):
HF5415.5.H6313   1990
658.8'12—dc20   90-8788
                                         CIP

90 91 92 10 9 8 7 6 5 4 3 2 1

Contents

Foreword

FRENCH companies, awakened by the successes of their American and Japanese counterparts, have become increasingly conscious of service quality. I am delighted with this new awareness and hope it will soon result in an overhaul of company structures and a universal adoption of quality policies.

Indeed, service quality has been the hallmark of our work at Club Med. Thirty-five years ago, we realized that service was the primary reason for our existence. Without unceasing, company-wide dedication to providing customer driven service, we would never have become the leader in our field.

We developed a rigorous service delivery policy central to everything we do, whether personnel training, the building of our international villages, or the error hunt for zero defect. This passion for service quality is closely linked to the implicit promise that we make to all our members: to make them happy. Service quality is the job of the entire organization. Employees, supervisors, managers, and all those who are in contact with the customer must cooperate in a vast, organized error hunt that will only reach zero defect if everyone subscribes with the same enthusiasm.

Buttressed by his double experience as teacher and practitioner, Jacques Horovitz echoes these priorities in this book. He demonstrates that in today's world no company can survive without paying attention to the customer and to the quality of the service that must be provided. The author has counselled Club Med on the integration of the service quality dimension. His vision will be useful in every business sector, including industry, as demonstrated by the many examples in this book.

Getting to the heart of the matter, Jacques Horovitz illustrates the importance of quality as perceived by the customer. He discusses methods that will enable managers to surmount the difficulties in attaining quality service and he does not hesitate to denounce the harmful consequences of a lack of quality (costs, poor reputation). He reminds us of the role of communications, both internal and external, in the success of a service strategy and he gets right down to details, from the welcome to advertising, and includes documentation and telephone behavior.

In order to hold their own in markets, which are increasingly competitive, companies are going to have to establish specific and detailed programs that focus on quality. For this purpose, Jacques Horovitz describes ways to launch a service quality program. By following these guidelines, the reader will be able to diagnose the status of service in a company, and, as the case may be, to improve or reorganize the quality policy.

At Club Med, we constantly remind ourselves that we must strive to satisfy the customer (after all, isn't the customer always right?), while anticipating the customer's needs and responding to his or her expectations. Jacques Horovitz illustrates this attitude with relevant anecdotes.

Knowing that a dissatisfied customer will relate that dissatisfaction to 11 people, while a satisfied customer will communicate satisfaction to only 3, it is evident that the good manager will pay special attention to "word of mouth".

In this book, Jacques Horovitz gives vital information on how to conduct practical satisfaction surveys that should be the starting and finishing point of each company activity.

I do not wish to reveal any more about the content of this book, but I would like to assure the reader that *Winning Ways* offers an original approach to service quality. This volume, with its generous and effective themes, will become an indispensable companion for managers at all levels in the conquest of zero defect, the real priority in today's competitive, international environment.

Gilbert Trigano
CEO
Club Mediterranean

Publisher's Foreword

AT A recent seminar, I asked the attendees how many liked to shop at large discount stores. Only one in a group of one hundred raised a hand. It seems these stores, with their faceless aisles and limited selections, have gone the route of "no-frills" air transportation. The age of volume discounting, at the sacrifice of service, has mercifully passed.

When I was a young boy, Main Street had a store for everything. There was a grocery store, a barber shop, a drug store, a five and dime, and a fish market. And who can forget the milkman who knew just how much of each dairy product we wanted for the week and delivered them to our door? These store owners and vendors knew all their customers, most by first name, and we knew them. Each of them took pride in their products and delivered them with the best service. If they didn't, they lost the respect of their customers and neighbors and they went out of business.

Once America expanded into a supermarket mentality, we lost this sense of service, this connection to the customer. But American consumers still want that. Surrounded by hundreds of options for each purchase they make, people seek

xiv • Winning Ways

out and pay for quality service. And there are a growing number of companies throughout the world that know how to deliver quality service. These are the companies who will succeed in the long run.

If a family buys a television set at a store where they received bad service, they remember the feeling they had when they bought it. Every time they turn the set on they probably talk about that rude salesman who wouldn't answer their questions. When the first thing goes wrong with the set, their negative feelings toward the salesman spread to the brand of the product and the store where it was purchased. Do you think they'll go back to that store for their next appliance? What do you suppose they tell their friends about that store?

The effects of bad service compound exponentially. Customers who receive bad service tell, on the average, 10 to 15 people. Customers who receive good service tell perhaps 3 others. By word of mouth, the customers receiving bad service will destroy the market edge of that company. As people gradually get the word that an alternative exists in the service-oriented company, that company will gain more and more of the market share.

In *Winning Ways*, Jacques Horovitz shows the reader by example and with statistics, why a commitment to quality service is the only critical factor for success in both service and manufacturing industries. With straightforward simplicity Horovitz shows how to design and implement a quality service strategy. Sales people, managers, CEOs of manufacturing companies, and everyone in the service industry will benefit from reading this concise guide to achieving "zero-defect service."

At the point of service, "there can't be any rejects," says Horovitz. "A factory can scrap 20% of its products if they prove to be defective. But it is not possible to scrap 20% of one's customers when they are unhappy."

Zero-defect service is Horovitz' term for "doing it right the first time," and he discusses how to find and eliminate errors in service delivery. In talking about defining service standards, he declares that "a standard is the result expected by the customer." In discussing how to design a service strategy and communicate that strategy to the customer, he points out that "where service is involved, everything is communication!"

This book includes examples of good and bad service and how to take advantage of customer complaints. And best of all, each chapter ends with self–diagnosis questions which lead the reader through a simple but effective process for implementing a quality service strategy. Continuous improvement methods, well-known in manufacturing processes, are here applied to the point of sale with great benefit to all those involved in customer interactions of any kind. I hope you read it, enjoy it, and apply it to your service delivery process.

I want to thank Jacques Horovitz for his friendship, for sharing his ideas at our conferences, and bringing his valuable perspective to our readers through the translation of this book. I am grateful to Camilla England for her efforts in acquiring this book. I also want to thank all those who helped bring this book to an English speaking audience. An excellent translation of the French original was provided by Cynthia Cash of Management of Strategic Resources in New York. Ms. Cash also helped coordinate our communications with the author. Thanks go to my editorial and production staff for preparation of the manuscript, to the people at Rudra Press for typesetting and printing, and to Micki Amick for the cover design.

Norman Bodek
President

Acknowledgments

I N THE way of acknowledgments, let me begin with two words borrowed from customer service:

"Hello" to the reader who is interested in service quality and strategy.

"Thanks" to the reader for sending me your comments, experiences and ideas.

To Danielle, who had faith in me.

To Charles, Mark, and Dago, who read and reread my manuscript and commented on it.

To Marta, who typed and retyped the text to zero defect.

To all the progress-oriented companies with whom I have spent time in the search for perfection and who have called upon me to create, develop, and reinforce their service quality policies.

I owe a special debt of gratitude to Club Med, that great service company which has always been in the forefront of quality. The GO (Gracious Organizer) spirit, with its generosity and attentiveness permeates each member, from the CEO to the sailing instructor. Club Med sells the most intangible of services: happiness. Its goal is to provide zero defect happiness for the GM (Gracious Member). Implementing a system to establish such an ambitious policy throughout the world has been a particularly interesting job for Club Med and for myself. The Club adopted the system, and the positive results were quickly apparent. Club Med's achievement of zero defect happiness should provide encouragement to other, more down-to-earth service providers. Spare auto parts dealers, data bank sales, and restaurants will find the quest equally exciting and fulfilling.

So, to everyone in business, from large scale retailing to hotels, from insurance to computers, and steel making too: Don't be afraid to seek zero defect service—for your customers.

Introduction

G LOBAL competition began when the Japanese introduced quality production into Europe and the United States. In 1981, American CEOs were still declaring that eighty percent of their products were of better quality than Japanese products. Eighty percent of American consumers however thought differently. The battle intensified with the introduction of concepts such as "zero failure", "zero problem", "zero deficiency" and "zero defect".

More recently, an offensive has been launched on the service front. Service before, during, and after product sale has become increasingly important. Banks, insurance companies, transporters, tourist agencies, government agencies, restaurants, and catering services are just a few types of businesses that have become concerned with service quality. The service war is especially crucial in Western economies, where services represent an increasing share of the gross national product (70 percent in the United States, 65 percent in France, 56 percent in West Germany).

Thanks to the combined effects of telecommunications and computers, concern with service quality will soon be global.

Indeed, these two technologies will create economies of scale in services and simultaneously provide large, multinational service companies with opportunities to create new markets. Competition will no longer be merely local or national but international. Finally, it will become possible to reconcile the irreconcilable. Thanks to advanced technologies, mass production will coexist with services adapted to individual customers, blending high tech with "high touch" (special attention to each customer).

Even as they are presented with these new opportunities, many companies continue to act as if they were in a market of scarcity. These companies do not appear to realize that international competition, in terms of service, will become tougher every day, but a number of Japanese, Swiss, Singaporean, Dutch, and Swedish companies have already realized this. The challenge of service excellence has now been launched worldwide. Many hotels, insurance companies, transporters, banks, data processing companies, consulting firms, travel agencies, and tour operators, as well as companies in such sectors as industrial cleaning, security, distribution, and food catering have already gone international.

Service quality and product quality, however, must be managed differently. Service is intangible. Unlike products, which are manufactured before being sold and used, service is created and consumed simultaneously. A number of techniques to manage quality developed by the manufacturing industry can be applied to service, but quality circles and the various error chasing methods are not enough to assure service quality. Quality management in industry increases productivity by reducing waste and lowering production costs. In services, productivity is expressed through customer satisfaction and is measured by increased sales.

The purpose of this book is to give managers of service companies and industrial companies for whom service is a competitive weapon the means to establish quality policies for the services they provide. In other words, it will try to point the way to service excellence. Its goal is not to create an awareness of the importance of the customer. Many books have already explored that subject. This book addresses the questions that naturally follow once the importance of the customer is accepted.

Methods do exist for managing the quality of services. I have tested them while assisting companies in diverse fields: restaurants, travel agencies, hotels, banks, large scale retailers, schools, computer services, spare parts dealers, and consulting firms.

The major principles upon which the quality of service depends, and those that will be developed in this book, can be summarized as follows:

- *Customers* are the only legitimate judges of service quality. Their *opinions* are of vital importance.
- *Customers* determine the service excellence level and they *always ask for more.*
- Each company must *formulate a promise.* That will enable it to satisfy its target clientele, while making money and distinguishing itself from the competition.
- The company must *manage the expectations* of its customers, minimizing the difference between customer expectation and company performance.
- *Service promises* must be converted into *quality standards.* Service quality is a very subjective idea. Nevertheless, precise standards can be defined.
- *Strict discipline* and *constant vigilance* are necessary to *eliminate defects.* In providing service there is no middle road. The goal must be perfection: zero defect. One can improve the quality of services by managing details.

- The quest for excellence demands a *universal commitment*. Everyone in the company must be involved, from the CEO to the newest employee.

Because every firm operates in its own universe, every effective service quality strategy will demand solutions unique to that universe. However, the principles stated above will be indispensable to the development of a service strategy, regardless of the internal and external circumstances of the company.

Each chapter in this book concludes with a Self-diagnosis, a series of questions designed to help the manager diagnose present service quality policy. I hope these questions will provide guidance, enabling the reader to understand present conditions, to identify strengths and weaknesses, and to forge an action plan.

Winning Ways

Achieving Zero-Defect Service

CHAPTER ONE

———

Quality and Service:
Some Definitions

*T*HIS BOOK is about understanding and managing ser-
vice quality. Since service quality is a very subjective matter,
it might be best to begin with a few definitions. Is there a single level of quality or are there several? How much does
quality cost? What exactly do we mean by service?

Quality

Quality is the minimum *level of service* that a firm chooses to
provide in order to satisfy its *target clientele*. At the same
time, it is the degree of *consistency* the firm can maintain in
providing the predetermined level of service.

The Level of Service

In the world of services, quality does not necessarily mean
luxury, supremacy or "top of the line." Management must
first identify the level of service to which the company will
aspire. A service reaches the required degree of excellence
when it meets the expectations of its target clientele, regardless of how that clientele is defined. If the customer segment
wants a repair person to visit within three days, there is no

3

need to provide one within three hours. Depending upon the target clientele in question, three days and three hours may be equally valid levels of excellence. McDonald's serves quality for two dollars. Caesar's Palace provides another level of quality, at another level of cost. The level of service should correspond to the values for which the customer is willing to pay.

The Target Clientele

The target clientele is the one that, by its expectations, its needs, or both, dictates the level of service to be provided. Today, industrial and consumer markets are more and more stratified by an ever increasing diversity of customers. A student and a business traveler may stay at the same hotel. But the student usually does not demand the same level of service as the business person. The Chevy shopper does not expect the same level of service that a Cadillac buyer expects. A law firm seldom demands the same quick repair time for its laser printer as a firm of architects.

Faced with the multiplicity of needs, each service must choose a target clientele. Yielding to the temptation to furnish a little bit of satisfaction to everyone is the surest way to fail.

Consistency

Consistency is the third parameter of quality. It demands the same level of excellence every day and everywhere. Guests cannot be received more cordially in the morning than in the afternoon. A restaurant chain cannot serve good food on the east side of town and mediocre food on the west side. Conformity to standards is the most difficult aspect of service quality management to maintain.

The more dispersed a service distribution network is or the longer the chain of go-betweens, the greater the danger of deviating from the established level of excellence. Companies that sell through intermediaries, such as insurers, microcomputer firms, or tour operators, have an even more difficult job: to maintain their own service quality to intermediaries and help the intermediaries to consistently provide a high level of quality to the eventual customer.

In the same way, the more the quality of a service depends upon employee behavior, the greater the risk of inconsistency. The big advantage of an automatic teller, for example, is that it is never in a bad mood.

Whether human behavior has a major or insignificant effect on a service, whether the service is delivered through numerous locations or intermediaries, reducing the gap between the service actually provided and the targeted level of excellence must be the goal. Long-term success can only be guaranteed by constant and consistent monitoring of every phase of the delivery program.

Disney theme parks are a model of consistency in their ability to deliver quality service. The service is equally commendable whether one visits Mickey Mouse on the east or west coast. But the Disney success does not just happen; it's the result of comprehensive and consistent planning, training, monitoring, and fine-tuning.

Service

Service is comprised of all the supports that the customer expects beyond the basic product or service that are consistent with the price, image, and reputation involved. The buyer of a Mercedes expects a certain number of services during and after the actual purchase, that is, a personalized reception, an extended test drive, tailored credit, fast repair or even zero failure, as well as the prospect of receiving top-dollar value at trade-in time. Likewise, when Hertz promotes its "#1" position, it commits itself to helpfulness, immaculate cars in perfect condition, and an immediate response to customer problems.

But service goes beyond friendliness or kindness. It is true that a smile is never superfluous. It is also true that a smile is "visible" on the telephone. But the smile must be accompanied by the right information, it must connect the call to the right person and not leave the caller listening to Muzak. Good service is a question of method and not merely one of simple courtesy.

Think about hospitals. Perhaps the most memorable characteristic of one hospital is the warm welcome one receives at the reception desk. At the second hospital is an exceptional physician—but he is in a bad mood. Most people would still prefer to be treated at the second hospital. But what if a third hospital could offer warm reception personnel *and* treatment by a superb physician?

Service does not mean servility. People tend to confuse the two. This explains the well-known attitude of certain sales clerks in department stores who make one want to buy —somewhere else. A moment of pragmatism. Without the customer, there is no company and therefore no pay check. And without service, there may be no customer.

Our parents, less spoiled than we , were well aware of this when they worked long hours in their shops, sustained by a single truth: "The customer is always right."

Service in a Product Industry

The service of products has two components:

- the degree to which the product is problem-free
- the added value the customer receives

Beyond the fundamental usefulness and technical performance of the product itself, these factors are of equal interest to buyers of automobiles, bulldozers, computers, widgets, and baby cribs.

The "Worry-Free" Factor

In addition to the price and technical performance of the product, the purchaser is interested in incipient costs. These are generally measured in nonmonetary terms and include the time and energy invested to:

- get delivery and repairs
- receive an error-free invoice
- operate the device
- understand how the product works
- use it at full efficiency
- efficiently contact the right person in case of a problem
- get rid of or resell the old device

The customer will also assess the monetary costs connected with obtaining and using the product:

- transportation
- installation
- maintenance
- downtime

A properly tuned service quality policy aims to minimize the extra costs and effort incurred by the customer. Achieving a product with no inconveniences attached is the goal.

The happy customer is the one whose computer work is taken care of when her computer is under repair. She is the one who, thanks to a confidential telephone number, can submit a problem or an idea to the right person, have her old computer equipment removed, and be helped during the start-up phase with the new equipment.

All buyers do not demand the same degree of freedom from inconvenience. Some choose to pay a high price for total service. Others prefer to pay less and take on part of the service themselves. Digital Equipment Corporation (DEC), which has become a leading player in the world of computers in less than 15 years, understands this principle very well. It offers a variety of service programs, from all inclusive (everything done for you), to simply providing parts (do-it-yourself).

The Added Value Factor

Smart customers look for added value. They already understand the technical performance of the product. The choice of supplier will depend on less tangible considerations.

There are different kinds of added value. The social status of ownership is an important one. A Mercedes appeals to the business person who wants to present an image of affluence and respectability. The Porsche meets the need for prestige. An IBM computer offers the psychological guarantee of "Big Blue", Macintosh attracts the "hands-on" user, the innovator, the entrepreneur.

Added value can take the form of problem solving assistance. By using this approach, a small American can maker, Crown Cork and Seal, beat the giants at their own game. The firm works closely with its customers to design and develop packaging adapted to individual needs that is lightweight, less expensive, more suitable for merchandising. Problem solving assistance is also encountered in high performance banks; each customer can invest his funds according to his needs, his means and his hunches.

Added value can include financial support,—help in securing credit, easy payment terms, arranging the sale of old equipment or material. It can also be built around after-sale support,—training, repair, guarantees, spare parts availability, continuity of the line, technical updating. Finally, added value can mean speed and flexibility—speed in delivery or production, perhaps the possibility of modifying an outstanding order.

A service policy, associated with a product, can be analyzed based on two parameters: the degree to which it is problem-free and the added value. Figure 1 provides a convenient way to track the service aspect during various sales stages.

A company must define its priorities before it can develop a service policy to support its product. For example, if a company chooses to distinguish itself by promoting a problem-free policy before, during, and after sale, it must provide the customer with effective service personnel, user-friendly documentation, start-up assistance, quick and complete delivery, error-free invoicing with clear references, and minimum cost for maintenance, repair, and downtime.

	Before the sale	Installation	After the sale
Degree of being problem-free			
Added value			

Figure 1. The Dimensions of Service Surrounding Products

Service in Service Industries

Unlike products, services have little or no tangibility. Services exist only in human experience. In most cases, customers of a service cannot express their degree of satisfaction until *after* consumption. Product services can be conveniently divided into two components: the extent to which the product is *problem-free* and the *added values* obtained by the purchase of the product.

Service in service industries also consists of two dimensions:

- the basic features sought by the customer
- the experience at the time when the service is consumed

When guests reserve hotel rooms, they are buying rest. When people buy insurance policies, they are seeking some form of financial security. Everything that accompanies the basic service becomes important. A play will only entertain if the seat is comfortable. On the other hand, a restaurant that aims for fast table turnover cannot satisfy the diner who has come to relax.

Basic Service Features

There is a modicum of service that any airline passenger or fast-food purchaser expects to receive. The airline passenger expects to arrive at a selected destination. The fast-food customer expects to receive a bag or tray containing something to eat. These are the basic service features involved in each transaction. History is replete with examples in which even basic dividends could not be delivered by companies supposedly doing business in the service sector. Fortunately, history also records examples in which basic services, when orchestrated in an innovative manner, can provide a service that is greater than the sum of the parts.

All airline tickets look pretty much the same. Most hotels look alike. But it was a unique combination of these elements, wrapped in a finely tuned service policy that Jan Carlzon credits for the tremendous success of Scandanavian Airlines (SAS). The company began by identifying business travelers as its target audience. It then rescheduled flights, added a business class, a special waiting lounge, luggage check-in service, and efficient credit card procedures to address the specific needs of business people. The results are history.

The Consumer Experience

Service in service industries can have a major impact on the consumer's experience and therefore determine the consumer's degree of satisfaction. An experience will be pleasant or unpleasant according to a variety of factors, including but not limited to:

- selection
- availability
- ambience
- attitude of the service staff (friendliness, courtesy, helpfulness, initiative) during the sale and while the service is being performed
- risk perceived in choosing the service that can be linked to the company's image and reputation
- other customers
- speed and accuracy of responses given to questions
- reaction to complaints
- personalization of services

When selling a service, the customer's first contact is particularly important. The location, staffing, and procedures of a check-in desk often leave one with a lasting impression of a hotel. The first contact between the customer and the company is even more important when the service will demand multiple contacts. A hotel guest, for example, encounters a room clerk, a bellhop, a housekeeper, a bartender. Each of these early contacts must be successful. If the early contacts are unsuccessful, there may be no later ones. The integrated nature of the two components is illustrated in Figure 2.

When customers were asked to rate the qualities that influenced their choice of department stores, they gave the following answers, in order of importance:

- The quality of the welcome: the friendliness of the personnel, the information desks, the signs, the ease of

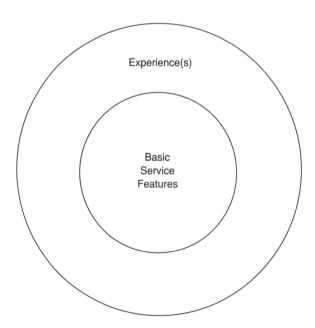

Figure 2. The Dimensions of Service in Service Industries

finding things and the advice from knowledgeable
sales people
- Convenience: access to facilities, easy circulation, purchase transaction speed, rest facilities, lighting and
ventilation, festive atmosphere, the pleasure of buying
- Choice: the availability and diversity of the items for
sale

The quality of the welcome proved to be twice as important as convenience and choice. Price and selection were sec-
ondary considerations. Welcome and convenience are
perceived through a number of features (e.g., lighting and
decoration) and from the experiences (e.g., atmosphere, circulation) that surround the act of buying. No big surprises here.
Why would one shop at a department store if not for the pleasure of the eyes, the ears, and the other senses? The customer
can find lower prices in discount stores and more personalized advice in boutiques.

Service can be just as important in banking and leisure industries. Can anyone resist the banker who offers a cup of
coffee in the privacy of an attractive office? Club Med owes
its success to the fact that it offers the opportunity to make
new friends, an easy going atmosphere, and freedom of
choice in sports activities. Its magnificent beaches and sumptuous buffets are less significant.

Quality is the level of service that a company attains in
order to satisfy its target clientele. It is also the degree to
which the company succeeds in conforming to this level of
excellence. Service is composed of all the supports that surround the act of buying. It is measured in terms of freedom
from inconvenience and added value for products, that is, in
terms of basic service features and the customer's experience
with the service.

Self-diagnosis

If your company is product oriented:

a) Make a list of the present service dimensions: the degree of freedom from inconvenience (before, during, and after the sale) the added value (before, during and after the sale).
b) Can you see other possibilities?
c) Do your competitors offer more?
d) Do the dimensions you've listed have different levels of importance for the various segments served?
e) Do you always comply with these levels? To what degree?

If your company is service oriented:

a) Make a list of the present service dimensions: the basic service features, the experience
b) Can you see other possibilities?
c) Do your competitors offer more?
d) Do the dimensions you've listed have different levels of importance for the various segments served?
e) Do you always comply with these levels? To what degree?

CHAPTER TWO

The Importance of Service Quality

C ONSUMER needs and aspirations for service quality are in a constant state of evolution.

The Customer Always Asks For More

Consumer studies agree that customers are increasingly demanding. But these findings don't tell the whole story. The perception of quality varies from one customer to another. Suppliers often have different views on service quality from their customers. Moreover, the quality of a service will be perceived differently according to whether the service is new or well established. The customer who has just discovered a service will tend to be less critical in his or her judgment than will the experienced user.

Toward Better Quality

Service quality has become a major factor in many purchase decisions. The reasons are manifold. Competition has intensified in most businesses, from tourism to data processing, from banking to the glass industry. The customer is being tempted with greater and greater service diversity.

Assuming parity in price, why should customers settle for a product offering less service?

Furthermore, the gluttonous consumer of the 1960s has been succeeded by a more selective and better informed gourmet. This trend has been exacerbated by the recent economic difficulties experienced by many Western nations and by a relative stagnation in consumer purchasing power. In a slow business climate service is an increasingly important factor in successful business strategies.

Stepping Up to Something Better

The customer's attitude toward service quality changes as the customer he learns more about a product or as his or her standard of living raises. In the beginning, the consumer is happy with a basic product, with stripped down service and low price. Gradually, an awareness of quality grows until the consumer demands increased excellence. Until Harley-Davidson grasped this principle the company suffered a tremendous loss in the market share.

Multiplicity of Experiences Increases
the Customer's Expectations

A customer may want increased service quality because buying behavior has been influenced by the difference between what is available at home and what he or she discovers traveling. A business traveler who spends time in Asia will be more demanding with regard to the service received in a domestic resort hotel than someone who has not experienced the charms of Asian hospitality. The tourist who has sampled the service quality of restaurants in Italy cannot resist comparisons to a favorite hometown eatery.

Customers become harder to satisfy for a variety of reasons. The computer specialist who has experienced Digital Equipment Corporation's after-sale service in the United States, will not fail to compare it to the service the same company offers to

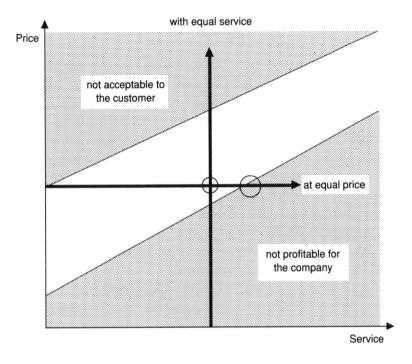

Figure 3. Meeting Points Between Customer and Supplier

its French customers. She will find the French service deficient and will not hesitate to complain. As borders open, as trade becomes more international, quality expectations grow. To remain competitive, companies must adopt standards to match their markets and stay abreast of what is happening in the rest of the service world.

The Japanese, for example, have a very strong tradition of courtesy, which they do not fail to employ in their conquest of foreign markets. It gives them a competitive advantage in countries where the customer is not used to being treated with deference.

Quality Conceived and Quality Perceived Are Rarely the Same

The superiority of a new service is always more evident to the inventor than it is to the potential customer. If the innovation deviates from the ordinary or if it amplifies a less tangible service, the gap widens. Every innovation encounters resistance to change, whether it offers a new dimension in the use of credit cards, automatic banking services, or automatic train ticket dispensers.

As a rule of thumb it is well to keep in mind that only 3 percent of potential customers are generally willing to act as "guinea pigs". These few are usually followed by trendsetters, who make up about 13 percent of the market. The bulk of the market will come around much later.

Quality should be the focal point of any campaign charged with communicating the comparative advantages of an innovation. Everything—brand image, reputation, guarantees, start-up assistance, user-friendly documentation, testimonials from satisfied users, ready availability of assistance personnel, and even the direct involvement of top management—must contribute to reducing the risk that might be perceived by the customer.

If You Want Something Done—Do It Yourself

Whether the product is new or well established, some customers will compare service quality to the savings they can enjoy by doing any servicing themselves. Do-it-yourself customers want a repair service that only charges for solving the problems that they can't solve. Some vacationers prefer to do most of their own planning and only use a travel agency for those details that they can't arrange on their own.

The Advantage of Being the Leader: A Dual-edged Sword

There is a common belief that a number one market position automatically creates a decisive competitive advantage. Asserting one's image and reputation can be advantageous. But look out! The more a company affirms its dominance, the more the customer will demand.

Number one benefits from a competitive advantage until the moment when, justified or not, it is perceived as being excessively dominant, arrogant, or impersonal. When the "leader syndrome" sets in, customers start to look elsewhere. Companies such as IBM, Xerox, or Hertz are aware of this. By constantly dominating, and by succeeding too well, one runs the risk of irritating buyers who prefer a bit more "modesty".

The Meeting Point

When prices are similar, the customer will choose the best service quality. When the quality is equivalent, the customer prefers the less expensive service. Figure 3 illustrates the meeting zone between the customer and supplier.

The Importance of Symbols and Information in Service Quality

The perception of quality is influenced by the environment surrounding the product. For example, fish always appear fresher when displayed on a bed of crushed ice. The ambience of an advertising agency waiting room and the appearance of reception personnel often serve as a clue to the creativity of the entire organization. The same factors are also strong indications of how the agency treats its customers.

Verbal and nonverbal signs can play an important role in packaging a service, smiling to express pleasure at seeing the client, calling the client by name, making eye contact in conversation, for instance. All these signs can contribute to a quality image.

Information can also have a considerable effect on the manner in which quality is perceived. A mediocre service can sometimes be excused if the user's perception is affected by an explanation of the reasons for the poor quality. When people waiting in line are told the reason for their wait, their aggravation is often tempered. This does not mean that Muzak should be responsible for keeping telephone customers amused. It is preferable to prepare a message that is appropriate to the service and to the customer, for example, travel information for a tourist agency, or an explanation of software innovations for a microcomputer manufacturer. The bottom line is simple: There is no substitute for a speedy, thorough answer.

The More Intangible the Service, The More the Customer is Influenced by Tangible Reference Points

The customer may have to refer to tangible elements in order to judge the quality of a service. The more complex and intangible the service is, the more the user will rely on immediately measurable criteria, in particular:

- The physical appearance of the place and the people: a doctor's competence is often judged by the neatness of the waiting room
- The price: the demand for quality generally increases in proportion to price
- The risk perceived: the customer who receives little information and assistance from the outset, or who must buy without a guarantee, will perceive a lesser quality in the service even when that perception is objectively erroneous

A product is evaluated in terms of its tangible and physical characteristics: the number of rooms in a house, its location, insulation, and amenities, for example. A service is more often appreciated for intangible factors: the experience of past customers, the warmth of the welcome, the clarity of the information, or the credibility of the company.

The Customer's Opinion Determines the Service Quality

Companies often misjudge the customer's opinion. Absorbed by the technical performance of their products and ignorant of the real motivations for buying, companies are apt to adopt unsuitable service quality policies. For example, a great number of firms promise a particular response time in case of machine failure, while the client is primarily concerned with knowing whether a replacement unit will be immediately available.

To maintain the desired level of excellence, it is essential to know that the perfume buyer is purchasing hope, that the vacationer is purchasing freedom from worries. A supplier may be marketing education, but the customer is buying practical training. While the agency is selling advertising, the customer is buying sales. While the producer is promoting a musical comedy, the spectator is buying entertainment.

Service Quality is Either Total or it Isn't!

When customers evaluate service quality, they do not dissect it into components. They judge it as a whole. They form an overall impression and seldom remember the relative success of specific aspects. Even more unfortunate, the customers tend to focus on the weakest link in the quality chain. They then blame the entire service for the faults of the single ineffective link. It is therefore essential, in a service quality policy, to ensure the utmost congruence among the elements. Whatever is offered, be it a product or a service, it will be judged on every aspect of its performance. A deficiency in any one area can result in failure for the entire system. That's why *service quality is either total or it isn't.*

It is pointless to serve a sumptuous meal on a paper table cloth, to sell a sophisticated quartz watch without proper instructions, or to install a high IQ telephone system without at least offering technical assistance. As products and services become available on an international scale, the congruence of the quality becomes an even more important competitive factor. If a company refuses to offer a certain service, a competitor may be waiting to capitalize on the refusal and develop its own competitive edge.

Congruence is not only ensured by extending quality to all aspects of a service, but also by ensuring consistency within the clientele. A service will usually get a favorable rating if customers note that the service's other customers are similar to themselves. "Customer portfolio" management is all the more important if customers meet at the point of purchase or consumption, as they do at recreation areas, large scale retail stores, and adult education centers.

Ignoring the congruence factor can have disastrous results. Witness the misguided efforts of the Paris Mass Rapid Transit System. In response to declining ridership, Le Metro launched its famous "Ticket Chic, Ticket Shock" advertising campaign. The point: It's chic to ride the subway and the low fares will shock you. After investing heavily in the advertising campaign the company neglected to spruce up the trains and the stations. For a few weeks the campaign seemed destined for success. Ridership increased. But once commuters realized that the Metro was no more chic than before, they deserted it for good. They figured one shock was enough.

The Concept of Quality Varies with the Culture

It is a common mistake to confuse quality with luxury. A five-star hotel is not the only standard of quality. McDonald's makes quality hamburgers. Quality is a ratio; it is the value obtained in exchange for the price paid. Furthermore, the various components of quality do not have the same weight from one country to another. For example:

- Punctuality: being ten minutes late in France is not as serious as in Germany.
- Attention given to the customer: at Colorado ski resorts, boxes of tissues are available to those awaiting ski lifts, an employee greets you at the entrance to the slopes, and another wipes the snow off the seat before you sit down; in Switzerland, a calculator is provided when you are changing money at a teller's window; in Japanese trains, you choose your seat and all seats can be turned to face the running direction of the train.
- The idea of honesty: an American-style handshake agreement does not carry the same weight in France or Italy.

Customer Satisfaction, A Secret to Uncover

Many elements influence the perception of quality and complicate an analysis of customer satisfaction. Understanding these influences is especially critical because customers often hide their dissatisfaction with service. The reason is simple. Most services are received on a one-to-one basis. From the customer's point of view, expressing displeasure can mean getting the faulty service giver into trouble. The issue becomes very personal and many customers shy away from confrontation. It is much easier to write a complaint letter about a defective transmission than about a clumsy waiter.

	Less Important				More Important			
	France	W. Germany	USA	Japan	France	W. Germany	USA	Japan
Punctuality								
Promptness								
Attention								
Exchange policies								
Personal warmth								
Courtesy								
Concept of honesty								
Quick response								
Accurate response								
Instructions for use								
Respect for the customer								
Asking customer opinions								

Figure 4. Primary Quality Dimensions Variables by Country

But customer silence is all the more serious for the company when the customer's displeasure with service may be very strong. Dissatisfied customers seldom grant the company a second chance. A customer dissatisfied with a first experience is almost always a lost customer.

Experience shows that out of 100 dissatisfied customers, only 4 will spontaneously express their discontent. It is essential that a company understand the degree of satisfaction of its customers. Comparing the number of complaint letters to the total number of customers served gives one indication. Setting an acceptable standard for complaints is a subjective process, but present opinion suggests that there should be no more than 800 complaint letters for every 100,000 customers served. That's .8 percent. If the complaint ratio rises to the 20 percent range, an alarm should be sounded.

A complaint ratio under 20 percent is not a reason for complacency. It might merely be an indication that customers don't know where to address their complaints. Customers may not take the time to inform the offending company of their dissatisfaction. But most will take pleasure in talking about it to friends and relatives. The Technical Assistence Research Program organization's market research puts it all into perspective. A dissatisfied customer will generally tell 11 people about a misadventure. The satisfied customer will seldom tell more than 3 people.

Self-diagnosis

- Who are your customers?
- Can you classify them into homogeneous groups?
- What services do they expect?
- By what criteria do they judge service quality?
- How do these criteria compare with their judgments of five years ago?
- Have they become more demanding?
- Have new criteria appeared?
- Have some changed or ceased to be important at all?
- What is the weakest link in your service delivery chain in your opinion? In your customers opinions?
- Do you know whether these criteria are different in the countries where you operate?
- To what degree are they different?

CHAPTER THREE

The Unique Nature of
Service Quality

THE QUALITY of a service is more difficult to manage than the quality of a product. A service generally has a greater number of visible components than does a product. There are many more elements to observe and evaluate about a department store than about an automobile. The customer does not see the bolt that holds the fender in place but will immediately sense when a cashier is having a bad day. It is generally accepted that a customer observes 10 service components for every product component.

Moreover, since customers tend to dwell on the least satisfactory element of a service, high satisfaction rates for services are particularly difficult to achieve. If the error rate is 1 percent on 10 service criteria, 1 percent of the customers will be dissatisfied to some degree. (See the explanation of conditional statistics below.) If the error rate is 5 percent, the proportion of dissatisfied customers goes up to 41 percent. If a service comprises 100 quality criteria, an error of 1 percent on each of them produces a 63 percent customer dissatisfaction rating. The risk of dissatisfaction increases as the number of service quality parameters increases. The more elements there are in a service, the higher the risk of error and the

---

CONDITIONAL STATISTICS

Error rates predicated on multiple variables demand special computation An error in any one component of a service compromises the integrity of the entire service. Thus, it is necessary to compute the possibility of being "right" at each step of the procedure. The measurement is made by determining the percentage of satisfied customers and multiplying it by an exponent equal to the number of variable. The result is subtracted from 100% to obtain the rate of dissatisfaction.

$$100\% - \left(\frac{\text{satisfied customers}}{100\% \text{ customers}} \right) = \text{rate of dissatisfaction}$$

Using data from the examples cited:

$$100\% - \left(\frac{99}{100} \right)^{10} = 11\% \qquad 100\% - \left(\frac{95}{100} \right)^{10} = 41\% \qquad 100\% - \left(\frac{99}{100} \right)^{100} = 63\%$$

---

greater the risk of displeasing a customer. Hence, it is simpler to manage service at McDonald's than to manage service in a three-star restaurant.

The duration of the customer contact also has a direct influence on the risk of error. The longer the transaction takes, the greater the risk of displeasing the customer. It is easier to control quality during a 24-hour hotel stay than during a month-long vacation. (See Figure 5.)

But the difficulties do not stop here. Service is temporal. It is often produced and consumed at the same time. A cheerful welcome cannot be produced, checked, stored. This being the case, one cannot "fix" service quality. Once the error has been committed, its moment is past and cannot be retrieved. Nor

The Management of Service Quality

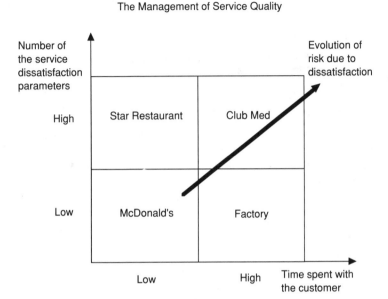

Figure 5. Evolution of the Risk of Dissatisfaction

can service quality pitfalls be easily anticipated. When a customer receives an incorrect insurance policy, it is too late to take it back and apologize. When a haircut goes awry, the barber cannot put the hair back. When a customer is sick after eating bad oysters, there is only one way to get relief!

The Management of Service Quality

Industry has developed methods to control product quality, but it is impossible to control the quality of a service after the fact. Sampling, inspection, and control are performed. But they are all done by the customer, *at the time of consumption.*

There can't be any rejects. A factory can scrap 20 percent of its products if they prove to be defective. But it is not possible to scrap 20 percent of a group of vacationers when they are unhappy. The simultaneity of service operations completely modifies the perspective from which quality is managed. In the manufacture of products, error prevention can lead to cost reduction. In providing service, error reduction is a direct guarantee of revenue.

A customer can't test a service before paying for it; the provider can't demonstrate the service without actually doing it. Deficient service can't be resold on the bargain table, nor can it be repaired or exchanged for good service. Hence, the vital importance of doing it right the first time. That's the subject of Chapter 7.

Because production and consumption of a service are simultaneous, the producer is not the only one who affects the quality. In service delivery the customer plays a direct and substantial role. Actors often perform better when they feel they're playing to a good audience. The success of a vacation cruise depends, to a large extent, on how well the passengers get along with each other. A computer data service can only provide top performance when used by customers who have taken the time to learn how to use it.

The elements of a service that can be affected by the customer must be disassociated from those over which he has no effect. One can control the quality of the former by handling them as industrially as possible. In a bank, for example, counseling services are affected by officer-customer interactions. But the same officer usually has responsibility for keeping accurate records of client transactions, balances, and so on. The maintenance of these records will not be affected by the client and should be managed in as efficient a manner as possible. This efficiency should enhance the customer's confidence in any subsequent interactions with that officer.

Geographical dispersion also adds to the difficulty of managing service quality. When two factories make a product for the world market, it is easier to control production quality than to control the quality of the hundreds of dealer networks and thousands of selling points that will eventually route the product to the customer. The broader the area over which the service is dispersed, the greater the risk of deviation from quality standards.

Cost of Quality Versus Cost of Lack of Quality

During the last decade many companies have expended considerable effort to improve the quality of products. Their goal has been to reduce costs and improve profits. By urging people to suggest ways of improving their work methods, managers hope to reduce inspection time, reworking time, and rejection rates. Instead of spending money to inspect, rework, or scrap a rejected product, some companies have invested in quality circles. Ideally, the quality circle will develop ways to improve product quality and find ways to save money. In the field of services, quality improvement offers little opportunity for cost reduction. On the other hand, the benefits of errorless service are considerable. Positive word-of-mouth publicity always leads to increased sales.

The standards for product and service quality are very different. A company builds 100 cars. If 10 are defective and require an extra investment equal to 10 percent of production cost, the total extra cost is 1 percent. A zero defect program will provide a maximum gain of 1 percent.

In the service sector, a satisfied customer passes her enthusiasm on to an average of 3 others. The Technical Assistance Research Programs (TARP) survey also determined that a dissatisfied customer communicates her aggravation to an average of 11 persons. Thus 1 percent of dissatisfied customers will generate another 11 percent of potentially dissatisfied customers.

The founder of the Marriott hotel chain talks about "50 million moments of truth". Every day, throughout the world, customers have 50 million contacts with the Marriott chain. The public has 50 million moments to test the company's ability to deliver quality. Each of these moments can create a satisfied or dissatisfied customer. If the customer is satisfied, he will tell 3 friends. If dissatisfied, he will tell 11.

Management of service quality often demands considerable investment. Since the service provider must do it right the first time, the investment actually buys prevention. But whatever the stakes, the cost of quality is generally less than the cost of the lack of quality, and the yield from service quality can be very high. First, today's advertising budgets prove that it is more expensive to win a new customer than to strengthen ties to an existing customer. Next, the manager must compare the investment in prevention to the costs of internal and external deficiency. A quality improvement program recently instituted by a large appliance distribution chain generated from five to eight million dollars worth of deficiency cost reduction. The program cost under $500,000, less than 10 percent of the savings generated.

Still more important is the fact that an investment in service quality is often a source of extra sales. (My experience, over nearly a decade, shows that every dollar invested in service quality produces an average of $100 in sales.) The gains result from a drop in dissatisfaction rate, the positive impact of word-of-mouth publicity (50 percent to 70 percent of people choose a service based on word of mouth), and the development of stronger ties with existing customers.

The stakes are enormous. Unfortunately, it is often difficult to convince a financial officer of the profitability of investing in quality. Manufacturing has learned to budget scrap reduction, but the service industries have only begun to recognize the importance of budgeting for quality.

The Total Cost of Quality
Can Be Broken Down as Follows:

- Costs of prevention: expenditures for preventing errors and for doing it right the first time.
- Inspection and control costs: expenditures to control quality. Merely performing audits does not accomplish much since the customer has already perceived the problems.
- Costs of internal deficiency: expenditures due to the lack of quality, such as duplicate invoice preparation, reimbursements, sending a letter of apology, plus scrap and rejects (forms, documentation to be redone) for all the tangible parts of the service.
- Costs of external deficiency: expenditures for convincing new customers to replace lost customers, counteracting negative publicity, and recovering the loss of business from customers who do not return.

Managing Service Quality Involves
People and Methods

Industry relies on machines to guarantee product quality. Automation, robotics, and computer assisted manufacturing and design have all played a role. In services, the efforts can only involve people and methods. *Service is a people business.*

A service company can achieve major savings by breaking down its service chain, standardizing delivery steps, simplifying and centralizing. The experience of Federal Express is exemplary. After having studied the risks of error during the various phases of routing mail, Fed Ex opted to centralize its operations. It built a center where mail is collected, sorted, and redistributed to the various regions of the United States. Federal Express's service is transporting mail quickly and to the right destination. By centralizing all the sorting tasks, the company found the way to minimize errors and soon gained a decisive competitive advantage. Centralization is a method that may be applicable to many other services. Maintenance and repair can often be organized from a single center.

Methodical error prevention through centralization also has an effect on the personnel department. A centralized company finds recruitment, hiring, training, and communication policies easier to control. It will also find it easier to rally personnel around the idea of quality and commitment.

Most American airlines have centralized reservation services. Local calls are instantaneously forwarded to a central reservation center where all operators use the same data base. The New York City fashion buyer and the Plano, Texas ranch hand both get the same answers. Thanks to modern data communications networks, financial institutions can also group their services. A major bank has developed a system for quickly answering requests for credit. Loan officers can directly access a central file. Naturally, centralization is more valuable when there is a predictability to the customers' requests. When the service must be tailored to the customer, decentralization is preferable. In banking for instance, trust department services should be available at branch offices. It is often necessary to break a service down into subservices, reserving a standard method for the simple and frequent components and a personalized approach for more specialized applications. The combination of people and method is therefore essential in managing service quality. Neither element can succeed on its own.

At Your Service

Consider the modern variation of the automobile service station. During the oil embargo of the 1970s, major oil companies decided to enter the retail business. Exxon, BP, Texaco, and others wanted to move their product at the lowest possible cost. (Some even suggested that they also wanted to cut out intermediate dealers.) The self-serve station was invented. They are now ubiquitous on both urban and rural landscapes.

The service stations feature well-lit signs, which can be seen for miles, and a large number of pumps, each equipped to supply three or four different qualities of gasoline. Customer can either pump their own (and save five cents a gallon) or drive into the full-serve lane and have the gas pumped by the attendant. The latter option typically includes two questions: "Look under the hood for you?" and "Windows ok?" (In the old days these services were taken for granted.)

After the gas has been pumped, by whichever option, the customer must leave the car and walk to the cashier's counter. The register is often encased in bullet-proof glass. On the way to the counter the stomach is tempted by a vast array of snacks, beverages, and caffeine pills. (For some reason popcorn and fried chicken are always prominently displayed.) There's a rack filled with comic books and magazines, in case the children are getting bored, and a drug shelf with aspirin, car-sickness remedies, and cold tablets. Somewhere in the rear of the building one might find a set of restrooms. The rest-rooms always come equipped with those disgusting hot air blowers instead of hand towels. (Hand towels must be harder to manage.)

After one's odyssey through the carbohydrate belt, the customer is greeted by an amplified voice (remember the cashier is encased in bullet-proof glass) hawking cigarettes, road maps, or oil. (If we don't ask about your oil, your gas is free!) Payment is exchanged via a pivoting drawer so that one need never come into direct contact with the cashier.

The system doesn't work badly if all the customer wants to do is stock up on 93 octane fuel, munchies, and soda pop.

But driving into this "service station" with a broken water pump is an entirely different experience. The man hired to pump gas for the infrequent full-serve customer couldn't find the water pump with a map. (He was hired to pump gas.) The cashier can't leave the register without setting off a burglar alarm. When asked about a mechanic, she offers that somewhere down the road there used to be one, "and 'round here, everybody goes fishin' on Wednesday". But she thinks he's in the hospital, or maybe he's out fishing. After all, today is Wednesday. The axiom that service quality has many levels is proven again!

What to do for the broken water pump? Try feeding it some fried chicken!

Self-diagnosis

- What is the satisfaction rate of your customers?
- How much does your average customer spend with you in a year?
- How much money did you spend on reimbursements last year?
- How much did you spend on audit, inspection, control? Among your dissatisfied customers, how many will never come back (if you are unable to estimate the figure, take 85 percent)?
- What are your total sales? What percentage do you stand to lose due to dissatisfied customers? How much would you need to spend (in advertising, sales force, promotion) to replace the lost customers?
- How many customers do you estimate will never come in due to negative word of mouth?
- What is the total cost of your external deficiency?
- How much do you spend to prevent service errors?

- Does your budget procedure permit you to justify increasing expenses to increase customer satisfaction (and the related contribution)?

CHAPTER FOUR

Service Strategies

MONOPOLIES are vanishing. Advertising strategies promoting "the newest model" and "the latest fashion" are shortening the life expectancy of goods and services. Technological improvements are making it easier to standardize the delivery of goods and services. Markets are becoming increasingly segmented and customers are increasingly difficult to satisfy. The company determined to succeed must develop a unique and durable competitive advantage. Today, such an advantage can no longer be ensured without a service strategy. In some areas, a service strategy may be the only way to attract new customers and strengthen the ties to existing ones.

This chapter deals with how a company can design a service strategy by combining existing know-how with market expectations. The process begins with questions. Does the firm want to become the Disneyland of recreation? The McDonald's or the Maxim's of food services? The Otis or the Xerox of after-sales service? The Thrift Inns or the Marriott of the hotel industry? The Swissair or the SAS of the airline industry? Each of these firms has succeeded in defining and implementing a service strategy that satisfies a particular market segment. In each of the cases the service strategy has given the company a unique competitive advantage. Swissair, for example, sells its passengers punctuality and safety, while SAS emphasizes traveling efficiency for the business traveler.

The Customer is King

This statement is seminal to the development of any effective service strategy. A company cannot exist without customers. In the search of a better bottom line many companies have lost sight of this basic truth. The illusion that a product will move off the shelves in any event has been refuted in most businesses. The "old days" will never come back.

Companies that have accepted the central importance of the customer will achieve exceptional results, even while functioning in depressed markets. In the furniture industry, the one stop furniture warehouses have won increased market shares in the last few years. The One-Stoppers organize the entire shopping experience with the customer in mind: central locations near interstate exits, acres of parking, extraordinary selection, low prices (made possible by extraordinary volume), delivery or take-it-home-yourself options, a play room for the children, and even a comfortable snack area where the customer can rest weary feet.

In another depressed sector, the garment industry, Benetton has developed a competitive edge. In 20 years, it has established 4,000 selling points throughout the world. The outlets are kept small to give one the feeling of shopping in a boutique, and Benetton is one of the rare sportswear makers to encourage the customer to handle the merchandise.

The customer must be the starting point of every service strategy. The objective of a good service strategy must be to hold on to existing customers while winning over new ones. It is vital to understand customer needs and to address them.

SURVEY OUR EXISTING CLIENTS
TO SEE WHAT THEY REALLY WANT.
NEW SERVICES, MAYBE NOT OFFERED BY ANYONE.

Companies that ignore this elementary principle don't stay in business long. It may shock some business leaders, but today's customer is no longer willing to adapt to inconvenient company policies. The company must adapt to customer needs. It's a good idea to consider investing at least one dollar to address customer needs for every dollar invested in advertising. If one is not willing to accept this, the advertising budget might best be paid directly to the shareholders.

There are two ways to capture a market sector: wage a price war or offer something unique and superior.

Competition on a Price Basis or on a Difference

As a general rule, most European companies are ill equipped to win price wars. Winning would mean reducing costs. In the cost/price spiral, there is always a competitor who thinks it can do better. That competitor may have access to cheap labor or, in the case of American or Japanese firms whose domestic markets are quite large, it may be able to benefit from the experience curve (i.e. lower prices to capture a market share that will subsequently lead to lower production costs). Price rarely provides a long-term competitive advantage, however. Even if a company succeeds in developing a radically new technology to reduce cost, imitators won't be far behind.

On the other hand, French firms do have the know-how that gives them an advantage in a competition based on difference. Restaurants and catering, gastronomy, perfume, fashion, tourism, recreation and resorts, and software design are all fields in which French companies have been able to capture major positions in world markets.

Among the tactics of differentiation, service orientation can provide a winning edge. Many banks are being forced to adopt a service orientation. Smaller, less cumbersome businesses are offering services formerly the exclusive domain of banks. Credit unions and savings and loans offer interest checking. Instant check cashing firms are competing on another front. Squeezed between dynamic competition and the astronomical costs of cash routing (due to superfluous branches and earlier transaction due dates), banks are rediscovering their customers who, in the meantime, have evolved a different perception of their needs for financial services.

Contrary to an idea that is still widespread in the banking world, the customer is no longer apathetic. A recent study demonstrated that 25 percent of customers switch banks in any five-year period. Their decision is motivated by displeasure—with services. Furthermore, more and more people have begun to spread their financial business among several banks. Old style banks could take a real beating.

Banks are beginning to hear from customers objecting to excessive charges for personal checking accounts. A few years ago one paid an average service charge of 10 cents per check. Some banks now charge as much as $1 per check. It's a self defeating strategy. The customer is being asked to subsidize the bank's inefficiencies, but gets nothing in return. That's why more and more people are switching banks. They are tired of long waiting lines at the drive-in window, annoyed with statements that arrive at mid-month, and with ever-increasing overdraft charges, and frustrated at not knowing to whom they can express their displeasure.

A service based battle means:

- In a product business: a battle over everything that the customer has the right to expect of the company in addition to the basic product—service before, during, and after the sale.

- In a service business: a battle for everything that concerns the service features and the experiences involved.

Examples of good service orientation: (BE SURE TO UNDERSTAND THIS CONCEPT)

- The sale of a computer is preceded by a needs analysis, accompanied by user-friendly documentation, by assistance at installation and start-up, and followed by fast and effective troubleshooting and repair.
- The sale of kitchen utensils in a department store is preceded by convenient parking, easy and pleasant access to the store, accompanied by knowledgeable sales personnel, wide selection, and culminates with efficient check-out, acceptance of credit cards, and appropriate packaging.
- A hotel offers a restaurant, a bar, a trained service staff, business services including at least a photocopier and a fax machine, currency exchange, an exercise facility, and an automobile rental office.
- A service oriented haircut is not simply shortening the customer's hair. It must be fast if designed for busy people; in the latest style, if aimed at the style conscious; complemented by a cup of coffee, if designed to meet a need for pleasure and relaxation.
- Financial trust service should include a warm and confidential welcome, skill in analyzing the customer's needs and answering questions, clear documentation concerning fees and performance, instantaneous information about the value of the portfolio, anticipation of future trends, and guaranteed follow-up.

An effective service orientation will identify the needs and expectations of a target clientele beyond the obvious qualities of the product or basic service. It should complete and reinforce the company's basic marketing strategy. In the future, every company will have to depend on a service orientation to attract and retain customers.

Product Service Strategies

Keeping the dimensions of price and service in mind, a product supplier has three strategic options (see Figure 6):

- the high-fashion strategy: very special high-priced service
- the custom-made strategy: personalized service at a reasonable price
- the ready-to-wear strategy: minimum service and low price

The three strategies often coexist in the same market sector, but each is aimed at a different market segment. The high-

Remember This is For Products

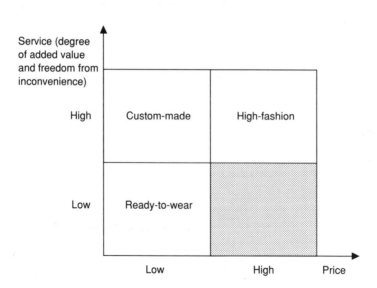

Figure 6. The Product Service Strategies

fashion strategy targets the customer for whom price has little importance, but who demands a "high touch" level of service.

The ready-to-wear strategy targets the customer who cares more about price than service. On the other hand, the custom-made strategy attempts to satisfy the customer who is sensitive to good quality service for a reasonable price.

All three strategies can fit within the product range of the same manufacturer. This is particularly the case in the automobile industry, where each major manufacturer has a model to appeal to every pocketbook and every life-style.

Certain products do not lend themselves to a service policy. That doesn't mean that creative management can't devise one. Whether one sells chemicals, electronic components, timber, or canned goods, an effective service policy can provide an edge. The celebrated American chicken king, Frank Perdue, found an edge. So did Crown Cork & Seal, the small manufacturer of aerosol and food cans. Starting with a slim 5 percent market share and facing competitors as powerful as Continental Can, Crown Cork & Seal now performs two or three times better in terms of margin and return on invested capital. How? By conducting a high-fashion policy with substantial added value. This company:

- concentrates on applications for which the container influences the quality of the content (e.g. pharmaceutical products)
- works in close coordination with research people from client firms in order to reduce the costs of using containers and packing
- provides customers with specialized machinery for filling and closing particular containers
- locates small factories near customers to ensure fast delivery and even opens factories throughout the world to follow its customers abroad

- reserves extra production capacity to respond to customers' last minute needs
- conducts surveys in supermarkets to pin point customer preferences

Crown Cork & Seal uses this data to propose better packaging ideas. Its customers are ecstatic. Who pays for the added value? Not the customer. Along side its service policy, Crown Cork & Seal rigorously controls its overhead and invests in the latest technologies to continually improve its productivity. Machines are often replaced, even before they're fully depreciated, so that the company can maintain its competitive advantages: speed, flexibility, and research.

A service strategy can also be implemented by orienting one's efforts toward being worry-free. Every manufacturer is interested in reducing costs due to machine failure, maintenance, and downtime. To an oil drilling crew a same day repair policy is priceless.

Many elements can be included in a product service policy. The customer can be aided in logistics, training, method changes, inventory accounting to minimize the costs of restocking or stockout, and even in the nature of the manufacturing process itself. Reaching zero hassle is a priceless goal. Alas, it is rarely achieved.

Service Strategy and Product Life Cycle

Even the best service strategy will change relative to the product's stage of development. Customer expectations evolve with the product.

Service is less important for an innovation. Concerned with the benefits offered by the innovation, an innovator may excuse service shortcomings. Since there is no equivalent product the customer has to take what he can get. For her part, the innovator generally prefers to invest in the development of the product itself. However, the customer may have a poor understanding of the product and perceive a risk in adopting it. A service with a high added value is appropriate: it might include start-up assistance, shared analysis of needs and applications, and follow-up. This will mean providing a service system.

During the growth phase, competition intensifies. To maintain the number one position, the innovator must now provide more and better service. A competitor may soon offer a similar product at a cheaper price. At this point the service must not only provide added value, it must also be more problem-free.

In the mature phase, the market may be saturated. Three different options must be considered:

- A ready-to-wear strategy: minimum service for a low price
- A high-fashion strategy: extensive service for a market that asks for it and is ready to pay the price
- An open-range strategy: choice of various levels of service

The last option has the advantage of serving customers with different needs; offering little service to the experienced customer who prefers to pay less while pampering the neophyte who needs extensive assistance.

Depressed industries may be limited to a few high fashion-target markets. Such a condition forces the most difficult decision: Fight it out on a price basis, or withdraw from the market. (See Figure 7.)

Service Strategies and Customer Value Chain

A service strategy can succeed only if the company coordinates all of the elements in the customer value chain. The chain might include any number of raw material suppliers,

Product development phase / Service strategies	Innovation phase	Growth phase	Mature phase	Decline
Dominant aspect of service	Value added	Problem free	Added value and problem free	High value added or withdrawn from market
Strategic options	High fashion	Custom-made	Ready-to-wear or custom-made	High fashion or withdrawn from market

Figure 7. Service Strategies and Life Cycles of Products

component manufacturers, intermediaries and dealers, and finally the customer. For example, to help a customer understand the applications for a product, it may be necessary to understand the materials that are incorporated into it at manufacture.

Serving the customer may require training dealers. Mistral, the sailboard manufacturer, continues to dominate the sailboard market by training its dealers, by making it mandatory for them to stock spare parts as well as finished products, by organizing the second-hand market for them, and by creating sailboard schools.

Service Strategies for Services

The relationship between price and service also exists in the service sector. However, the worry-free and added value dimensions are replaced by basic service features and experience.

In the service sector there are also three strategic options:
- the gastronomy option: high price and service
- the formula option: custom-made service at a reasonable price
- the fast food option: minimum service at a moderate price (see Figure 8.)

In the service sector the level of basic service includes two elements: the intensity of the interaction between the supplier and the customer and the duration of that contact. The "gastronomy" option targets customers who seek highly personalized service—a great deal of interaction and long contact. Alternatively, the "fast food" strategy seeks to satisfy the customer who is price conscious. This customer buys service with minimal interaction and a short contact period. Figure 9 positions four types of customer treatment in which the service is very different in intensity and duration of contact.

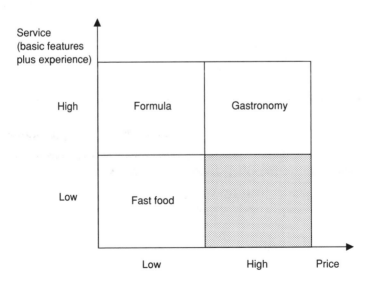

Figure 8. Service Strategies and Product Life Cycle

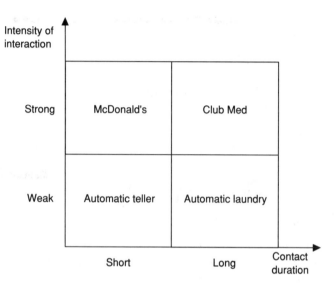

Figure 9. Basic Features that May Vary According to the Nature of the Service

The more the service supplier wishes to intensify the interaction with the customer, the more it must personalize the service. On the other hand, if it wishes to reduce the cost of the features, it must seek ways to increase standardization.

Therefore, the choice of a basic service strategy must be based on the possibility of standardizing and personalizing individual features. These two factors will give the features high or low service density. (See figure 10.)

Most types of features can be covered by different strategic options. As with industrial products, the different strategies can coexist within a service sector, as long as they create unique and durable competitive advantages. The variety of restaurants listed in the yellow pages proves the point. It is more difficult to imagine similar diversity in health services or management consulting. Health services have traditionally

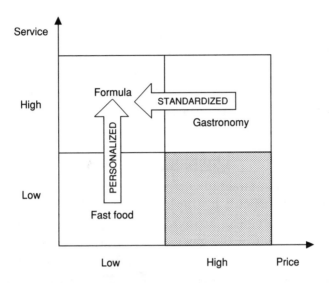

Figure 10. Strategic Options for Services

been delivered according to a gastronomy policy, with costly and highly personalized service (strong interaction between doctor and patient, long contact duration). But the recent proliferation of emergency 24-hour, health care centers indicates that even the medical profession is open to innovation. In the United States, day clinics have even begun to offer automated health diagnosis and will perform appendectomies without hospitalization.

The Gastronomy Strategy *(our level / clients)*

The gastronomy strategy is the most personal; it lavishes attention on the customer and serves him or her over a longer period of time. It assumes high costs and targets a limited market. This does not mean that the company that opts for this strategy will not try to reduce costs and increase productivity. On the contrary.

The advantage of a gastronomy policy is that the company can maintain the high level of personalization. Conforming to the level of excellence is the key factor in the success of such an approach. Many believe that the gastronomy strategy can only apply to luxury items. This is not necessarily the case. A printer can offer up-scale service, as can a dry cleaner or a building caretaker.

The Formula Strategy

The formula strategy is the most ambiguous strategy. It is often more difficult to implement than the gastronomy or fast-food strategies. It involves targeting a market that is larger than that of the gastronomy strategy, while still offering personalized service. Prices will be established to appeal to the widest number of people. Here, the trick is to conceive methods that are less expensive (lower contact cost), but that still personalize service. There are some interesting examples.

The Club. The club idea is still new in European management circles. The customer becomes a member of a group and as such benefits from various advantages. Since the group generally shares common interests, marketing is done by word of mouth and promotional costs are minimized. Club services (newsletter, special offers, and so on) personalize the service while at the same time standardizing it. The club formula is very promising but it has its pitfalls. Too much success can be dangerous. If the club gets too large, it becomes impersonal and the benefits of the club can be lost. An increasing number of service companies are using the club idea; automobile rental agencies, airlines, and mail order financial services head the list.

Information. Many companies are succeeding in reducing capital costs, without adversely affecting service quality, by employing sophisticated communications technologies.

Benetton, for example, never leases retail spaces with more than 600 square feet. All the merchandise is on display and the company avoids paying premium prices for on-site storage space. But thanks to a very sophisticated telecommunications system, Benetton can respond instantaneously to customer demand.

Standardization of know-how. Consulting firms know this approach well. It consists of developing a specific body of knowledge, then detailing and standardizing analysis and communication methods. It has numerous advantages. The consulting firm amasses a unique body of knowledge that distinguishes it from the competition. Once the wheel has been invented, the firm doesn't have to keep reinventing it. With a new coat of paint the same wheel can serve a number of applications.

This is also an excellent way in which to control quality and conformance with a desired level of excellence. Standardization also facilitates the training of newcomers. Finally, it provides cost efficiency. If every employee works in a standardized system, one can often make better use of junior, less expensive personnel. This is called a pyramid of skills.

Standardization of methods, training, and communication can be applied to many business sectors. A travel agency might develop an approach that would allow new employees to handle simple questions and more experienced staff to do travel counseling. Once the method is defined, judgment calls are minimized. So is the possibility of inconsistency. That will translate into increased profits.

Increase customer participation in providing the service. A company may also train the customer to play a more active role in the service. Telephone companies educate their customers to choose certain time periods. Restaurant managers opt for salad bars where the customer is invited to "make-your-own". Hotels place shoe-shine machines next to the coffee machines, to the great satisfaction of the guests. Computer manufacturers train their customers to manage spare parts inventories and to perform in-house maintenance. But watch out! The border between the formula and the fast-food options can get blurred. The more the customer is led to intervene, the less personalized the service becomes, the greater the risk of losing the customer. Nothing substitutes for a good understanding of customer needs and expectations.

The Fast-food Strategy

By maximizing standardization and minimizing contact duration, the fast-food service supplier reduces costs and therefore prices. It appeals to a market that is more concerned with price than with the level of service. Kitchens in institutional restaurants, for example, are shrinking. Precooked dishes, reheated in microwave ovens are replacing the enormous kitchens where armies of cooks once tended hot stoves.

Mail order firms offer catalogs that seriously rival shop windows (some of which don't dare to display their prices). And each of us has another new friend, the automatic teller.

Service Strategy: A Promise

A service strategy is always based on a promise made to the customer. McDonald's promises quality, speed, and cleanliness. Club Med, happiness. Sears Roebuck, choice and dependability. Holiday Inn, easy access at a reasonable price. The firm that chooses to compete on a service front must design a promise based on the needs of a target clientele, communicate it clearly, and above all, be faithful to it.

If the promise can be expressed in less than 100 words, it is a good sign. It's a good indication that the company is service oriented. If it can be stated in less than 50 words, the company has every chance of becoming the leader in its field. If the promise fits into 25 words, the company can't help but make a fortune.

The formulation of the promise is the responsibility of top level management. The promise formulated by top management will provided the basis upon which middle managers will define specific service standards. Several examples of promises made by successful businesses follow.

Swissair promises that the customer will always

- be transported in modern aircraft
- be transported in the safest possible manner
- receive traditional Swiss hospitality
- receive a dynamic response to customer needs
- receive assistance in the coordination of travel needs, even when the arrangements demand the service of outside providers

Swissair does not promise the most modern fleet, merely a modern fleet. Singapore Airlines replaces its aircraft every two years and assures this in their promise. Swissair does not say "anticipate needs," but "a dynamic response to needs." Incidentally, Swissair was the last European airline to introduce the business class.

Club Med promises that the customer will always

- be housed in a facility that is attractive and clean and where everything works
- be served with attentiveness, generosity, and imagination
- eat and drink according to personal taste; "all you want, when you want."
- make new friends easily and learn something new
- vacation without worry and without danger
- enjoy the village from the moment of arrival

Domino's Pizza promises that the customer will always

- be able to place a telephone order
- receive a hot pizza delivered in 30 minutes or less or deduct 3 dollars from the cost.

The first purpose of a promise is to facilitate internal communication. Every employee must understand the strategy, in terms of customer benefits. If the goal is universally understood, it will be easier to achieve. Only after management is secure in the knowledge that all employees understand the promise, should the same promise be offered to the customer. An unkept promise is worse than no promise at all. At the very least the company must commit itself to keeping it; to providing guarantees that fulfill the commitment or indemnify an unkept promise.

Finally, there can be only one promise for each target clientele. Each customer has his or her own needs and expectations. Even if a promise is well formulated and kept, it will not succeed if it is addressed to customers who don't want or need it. Keeping the promise must be a company-wide effort. The entire organization must dedicate itself to the promise, from procedures to people, from finance to communications. A company may have as many distinct organizations as it has promises. Banks, traditionally organized by product, are reorienting themselves by market and within each market (institutions, companies, individuals) by market segment. IBM, 50 percent of whose sales come from services, understands the premise very well. It recently instituted a reorganization by industry.

At the last Paris data processing show, a young French software firm "promised" a software program capable of transcribing handwritten text into a word processor language. Thinking about my manuscript and my terrible handwriting,

I was quick to ask: "How much does it cost? I would like to
have one; when can I have one?"

Nobody could answer me. I hope, for the firm's sake, that
it will deign to sell its product before people have to drop to
their knees begging. I would not be surprised if, one day, the
invention wins the annual French invention prize. However,
given the lack of a service strategy, I, like many others, will
probably buy the American or Japanese brand.

Self-diagnosis

- What are your various market segments? (LONGZ I, II, n
III)
- What does each of them want?
- What strategy have you chosen to service them: gas-
tronomy, formula, or fast-food?
- Have you defined promises to your customer?
- How is each promise expressed?
- Does the promise match what the customers want?
- Is it written in terms of results for the customer? Does
it make you unique?
- Does it contain less than 100 words?

CHAPTER FIVE

Communicating the Service

C OMMUNICATION plays a central role in the success of a service strategy. It is indispensable for broadening the client base, increasing fidelity, motivating personnel, and giving them a precise understanding of the chosen quality standards. Communication must be accurately targeted. It loses all effectiveness when it tries to be everything to everyone. Finally, communication is not limited to an advertising message or technical documentation. It covers *all* direct and indirect circumstances that bring the customer into contact with the company.

Emphasize the Difference

Communication is the only way to declare one's difference. Effective communication sends a message to the customer, associating product and service, basic features and service experience. Singapore Airlines advertisements always feature young, smiling Singaporean women. The customer is supposed to associate Asiatic graciousness and hospitality with the airline. The Arrow Shirt man, the Marlboro man, and the starlet selling perfume encourage the viewer to make similar associations.

The communication itself can be a means of differentiation. Lufthansa states that it is a German company. It sells organization, punctuality, and efficiency. At Lufthansa, service means anticipating problems. The advertisement picturing two technicians in front of an aircraft, captioned: "At Lufthansa, the service begins long before your first cocktail," says it well.

Finally, communication is a powerful tool for managing the expectations of a target clientele. Airline commercials often show happy senior citizens. Many senior citizens are apprehensive about flying. Seeing their peers enjoying a flight experience serves to lessen the fears. Television networks promote the presence of a woman in the broadcast booth for a football broadcasts. The message: women will also enjoy sports. The pick-up truck is depicted as part of the social scene. In the opening shot, the commercial shows the truck hard at work on the farm. In the closing shot a couple is going to the symphony in the same pick-up. The message? A pick-up can be stylish, too.

Mold the Customer's Expectations

Most customers have a preconceived notion about service quality. Favorable or unfavorable prejudices can be influenced by communication. In one famous restaurant, the top of the menu announces: "Cooking is an art and art is composed of patience." The impatient customer is no longer in a hurry.

There is a natural temptation to downgrade customers' expectations, so as to agreeably surprise them when the service is rendered. A bad idea. But it can be just as harmful to inflate expectations.

Promising Less

If the promise communicated is inferior to the service, one runs the risk of missing the appropriate customer and attracting an unsuitable one who finds the lower service promise attractive. Promising "speedy repair," communicates a lesser service than "repair within 24 hours". The less sophisticated customer may be pleasantly surprised, but knowledgeable customers will buy from the competitor who promises a more specific repair time.

Promising More

A promise that inflates the customer's expectations gives rise to potential disappointment and can result in terminal desertion. Singapore Airlines makes certain that only female flight attendants serve passengers. After all, it promises attractive, Asian hospitality. The male flight attendants work in the galley, unseen by the passengers.

Reduce the Risk Perceived by the Customer

The risk involved in using a service is always a major concern. It is not enough to reduce the risk by compiling a wide range of accompanying services. It may be necessary to address the customer's fears. Word of mouth and a company's reputation can be important to the hesitant customer. A company's specifically designed communication can also have an influence on the customer's perception of the risk. The message may speak directly to the customers fears. It may be more subtle and quote references and describe successful experiences. Another approach is to strengthen the firm's public profile. This option reassures potential and existing customers of the permanence of the firm.

Make the Service Tangible

If product-oriented communication must address intangible attributes, the opposite is true for a service. Whether it be an automobile or a household appliance, a consumer product is seldom purchased exclusively for its technical performance.

A product can also provide prestige, fulfill a dream, or create some other psychological advantage that only communication can convey.

The Oldsmobile campaign ("This is not your father's Oldsmobile") suggests that the aging Olds owner will feel young again. Lincoln Continental ads guarantee that the owner (and his car) will stand out in a crowd, even if the crowd is composed of luxury car owners. Anderson-Little (window and door manufacturers) commercials all begin in a 1940s setting. An old school bus brings the children home. There's an inner-tube swing hanging from the maple tree and Mom is in the kitchen making an apple pie from scratch. Of course, the viewer sees everything through an Anderson Window. When the scene changes to the present, the window remains a constant. Message: Anderson Windows stand for the same values and securities that the viewer associates with the innocence of the 1940s.

Services are generally intangible. Their messages must communicate advantages through tangible means. If the customer seeks the exotic, a photo of palm trees along a white sand beach may be satisfying. If the promise includes opulence at a moderate price, a photo of sumptuous buffets may address the customer's wants. Visual communication takes on a special importance for services; it comprises the tangible evidence of the promise. But it must be credible, coherent, and followed up by a service that fulfills the promise.

When Service is Involved, Everything is Communication

The effect of a glittering, full-color newspaper ad is negated if the customer is greeted in shabby surroundings. Keeping a service promise can be very difficult. It demands constant effort and mobilization of all the resources of the company. One weak link in the chain will disappoint the customer, and the entire chain will take the blame.

Every aspect of a service company should contribute toward communicating the company's unique position. Advertising is only part of the package. The graciousness of the receptionist, the telephone answering service, the speed of access to an account executive, the handling of complaint letters, the decor of the premises, as well as the appearance of the company vehicles, and the manners of the personnel, will all play important roles. In the field of service, everything is communication.

The Elis-Europe company rents linens. Its trucks are always brand new and meticulously polished. The customer concludes that the same can be said about Elis's linens. Similarly, a renowned Paris bakery delivers its pastries in a van that looks like a huge, pink gift box. An excellent signal! On the other hand, the Terminix pest control people have mounted huge, plastic bugs on the cabs of their service trucks. One would think that it's the exterminator's job to get rid of pests, not to bring along giant ones.

Sears, America's leading retailer, has very attractive television commercials. They promote selection and, for many products, lifetime guarantees. But many Sears stores are large and impersonal. The only visible employees operate the cash registers. That is little solace to the novice who's trying to buy a tool to fix a leaking faucet or the husband interested in surprising his wife with a gift of lingerie.

Not long ago, UAP (the French insurance group), adopted the slogan: "Being number one gives us special responsibilities." Shortly thereafter the company put one of its rental buildings on the market. It gave its tenants the option to buy their apartments. Many tenants wrote to ask for additional information. Their inquiries were never answered. Two months later tenants received letters notifying them that their options had expired. It apparently never occurred to the company that tenants might also need insurance.

Service by Telephone: A Powerful Way to Strengthen or Weaken a Company's Level of Excellence

Many companies do business exclusively over the telephone. For most others, the telephone is an indispensable resource. The image of a company and its services is communicated in the most literal sense in each of its hundreds of daily phone calls. To ensure the level of excellence that the company has promised to provide, the following fundamental questions must be answered: Who answers the telephone? How? How quickly? In what tone of voice? Are calls efficiently routed? Is there an answering machine or answering service after hours? How are complex questions handled? Are customers annoyed at the choice of "hold music"?

Telephone service must be managed with the same care as manufacturing or accounting. First, one must prepare a list of the parameters that come into play from the moment the receiver is lifted. For each of the parameters, a quality standard must be specified. The quality of the service for each parameter will be measured by the standard. The manager can compile data tracking: the number of lost calls, the average number of rings before answering, the average time the customer must wait before getting an answer or reaching the appropriate extension, and the number of written or verbal complaints about the professionalism of the person answering the phone.

A "telephone smile" is not enough. The company's telephone system should be constantly monitored to make certain incoming lines are sufficient to handle volume, that the while-you-were-out message system works efficiently, and that inquiries are answered in a timely fashion. Remember: An exasperated customer can easily become someone else's customer.

The Welcome: An Encounter that Goes Beyond the Reception Desk

It is often and wrongfully supposed that a welcome policy consists of placing an attractive receptionist along side an immense bouquet of flowers. A welcome takes place every time the company comes into contact with the customer, in or outside of its facility. The welcome can have many variables: a visit to the customer's home or a business appointment at the company headquarters or at a dealership.

Here again, a smile is not the only parameter. Calling the customer by name, dressing according to the nature of the service, and punctuality are all factors that raise the level of service excellence of the welcome. A good bartender sends a signal when a regular customer enters the bar. A slight nod tells the regular that he or she is recognized and welcome. The little gesture is even more appreciated if the bartender is busy mixing a drink. A receptionist can send a similar recognition signal to an incoming customer, even while she is on the telephone. One needn't actually say "Good morning" to each incoming customer (as is done on every floor of a Japanese department store). It would also be helpful to train reception personnel to interrupt their conversation when a customer arrives, without giving the impression that the customer is the interruption.

Documentation, the Pauper of Communication in Services

It is striking to note that service companies generally give their documentation an importance that is inversely proportional to the importance given by manufacturers to their products.

Bankers, car rental firms, restaurants, and consultants should regularly review their documentation to make certain that it remains consistent with their service promise. Retailers should pay similar attention to catalogs, invoices, and letterhead. All documentation should reflect the level of excellent stated in the promise.

The skeptic remembers her experience with her pension fund provider. At the time of the sale, the skeptic received a gorgeous brochure, full of promises. But once she's signed up, all she receives are anonymous photocopies demanding instant responses. A magnificent example of inexcusable communication!

Dependence on Dealers

The problem of communication is more complicated when the company does not have direct contact with its customer. Such companies must make certain that the communication performed by the dealers conforms to the desired level of excellence. This can be difficult because the dealers, who may not always be exclusive, may have their own priorities and opinions.

One of the ways to make the communications conform is to negotiate joint actions with the dealers. This collaboration naturally depends upon the relative strengths of the parties. The better the company is known to the final customer, the easier it will be to convince dealers to cooperate. The main thing is to make the dealers understand the quality standards and convince them that it is in their own interest to ensure perfect homogeneity with the service promised.

To ensure a continuity of image in the United States, Club Med convinced travel agencies to allocate part of their commission to joint ventures. The Club built an administrative training center where it has sponsored training programs, and conducted advertising conception and direct marketing campaigns, all with agency in-put and cooperation. It found a way to standardize documentation. Participating travel agencies sacrifice part of their commission in exchange for increased sales. The process works at both ends. The company protects the coherence of its communication policy.

This chapter discussed the value of communications and their potential influence on customer expectations. Internal communications are equally important to the development of a sound service strategy and are discussed in the next chapter.

Self-diagnosis

- What is your target market?
- Do you tend to inflate your promise or to deflate it?
- What are the real relationships between your service and what you communicate to your customer?
- Is the intangible made tangible? How?
- Do your telephone answer, your welcome and reception, your sales and nonsales documentation, your offices and vehicles, your answers to complaint letters, the skills and manners of your dealers measure up to your advertising? Do they make your service more tangible or do they leave many questions unanswered?

CHAPTER SIX

Service Quality Standards

*I*NDUSTRY measures performance in units, watts, joules,
inches, or pounds. The measurement of service quality has
not yet developed a similar standardization. Some industries create operating standards that have little to do with
the customer's interests. Hotels may have standards for setting a table, waiting on tables, or making a bed. These data
relate more closely to a Taylorist tradition than to quality
management.

It is critical to develop service quality standards in order
to verify performance and to determine whether a promise is
kept. In order to be operational, quality standards must be

- expressed from the customer's point of view
- measurable
- used from the top to the bottom of the organization

A Standard is the Result Expected by the Customer

To become a true performance indicator and not simply
an operational rule, a standard must be defined in terms of
results for the customer, that is, the customer shall have__,
the customer expects__, the customer wants__,. The next

step requires identifying the tasks that must be performed to satisfy the customer, that is, reception personnel must__, the hostess will__, the repair person will__.

Once the tasks are specified, and only then, can the manager develop methods for accomplishing the tasks.

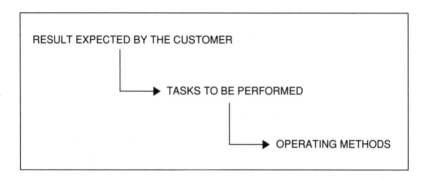

A service quality standard must be based on customer needs. It's the only way to guarantee conformity. Every employee should know what to do, how to do it and, particularly, why it's important.

Hotel guests generally appreciate a personalized welcome. Marriott hotel bellhops have been instructed to involve guests in conversation whenever possible. They are instructed to take special note of departure stickers on the customer's luggage. This information provides an instant entree to conversation.

A number of magazines send new subscribers a pamphlet entitled: "Everything you need to know to enjoy your subscription." The document describes a number of service quality standards concerning the mailing label, address changes, subscription and invoicing procedures, and options concerning sale of subscriber lists. The codes used on the mailing label are explained so the reader can see at a glance when the subscription is approaching its renewal date. The subscriber is promised that an address change will take less than four weeks and that the process will taken even less time if the subscriber calls the relevant information to an 800 number. The magazine is guaranteed to arrive no later than four days after it appears on the newsstands. By returning an accompanying post card, the subscriber will be removed from mailing lists that are regularly sold to a variety of marketing services.

The standard defines the tasks designed to satisfy the customer. Nothing prevents a business from doing more. Elvia, the French insurance and travel assistance company, sends flowers and a get well card to vacationing policy holders who have returned to France due to illness or accident. They do so even though a vacation insurance policy costs as little as $20.00! It's astonishing that real estate agencies, which collect huge commissions from residential sales, don't make similar efforts to thank new home buyers.

The Standard Must be Measurable

Conviviality, graciousness, and friendliness are difficult to measure by quantitative standards. But quantification is not always necessary. First, it's important to know whether a quality actually exists. A smile is not measured by its length but by its presence. A measurement may be a ratio or it may be expressed on a continuum. Nevertheless, one must try to break down service behavior into quantifiable elements. The speed of a function should be measurable in hours, minutes, or seconds. Courtesy is more difficult. Did the customer receive a "Good morning" or not? Was he or she asked how things were going? In some services, the welcome is the main cause of customer satisfaction or dissatisfaction.

Mr. Goirand of the Westminster Hotel offers the following wisdom: "To welcome someone, is to recognize him and to give him hospitality. The guest has traveled. He has come from far away. We need to simultaneously calm him and show him that he has come to the right place."

Recognition and hospitality are two elements that are measurable. They consist of a number of identifiable components:

- a smile: showing signs of pleasure at seeing someone
- verbal communication: greeting the person, knowing his name, speaking to him about his home town
- communicating with gestures: all the signs that signify recognition of the guest and confirm her welcome (avoiding turning your back to her or blocking her way, for example)
- visual communication: all the physical elements that enhance the guest's feeling of security and well-being, such as direction signs
- written communication: brochures and folders, each document in the guest's language, easy to read and understand—the hotel registration card, the travel agency brochure, the furniture dealer's catalog, or the policy issued by an insurance company
- the competence of the people providing the welcome: their ability to answer the guest's or customer's questions and solve any problems that may arise
- tangibility of the welcome: a warm and comfortable welcome, appropriate to the service supplied—It would be unnatural to seat a McDonald's customer in a leather armchair, just as it would be incongruous not to install a telephone in the guest room of a five-star hotel
- continuity of welcome: reception is not limited to a first contact, everything must continue to welcome, from check-in to sales, from the invoicing service to the repair service

When a welcome is broken down into its various elements, it becomes obvious that it's more than a question of properly greeting someone. Some people will do it better than others, but a welcome *is* something that can be learned.

Sometimes a welcome involves no human contact. This type of welcome should be easier to control!

Try finding a small town once you get off the interstate anywhere in the South. Fork Union is listed on the exit sign and it's even listed on the sign at the end of the feeder road. Three miles down the road a sign announces the way to Creed, Short Pump, and Mineral. But what happened to Fork Union? (The map, securely tucked in the glove compartment knows that Fork Union is six miles past Putneyville, which everyone around here knows is just down the road from Mineral.) Next adventure: a fork in the road. Short Pump, Mineral, and Putneyville are to be found down the right fork. Dixie and Jackson are advertised for the left fork. But where's Fork Union? And then, surprise! Your perseverance and your lucky guess at the fork pays dividends. A sign hidden behind an overgrown wisteria bush says that Fork Union is that-a-way. Ten minutes later one is treated to a "Welcome to Fork Union" billboard that is half covered over with Rotary, Kiwanis and Ruritan logos. While being welcomed to Fork Union the traveler begins to wonder how long it took the bill board company to locate the place to stick the sign.

The less a service depends on human behavior, the more important it is to define and quantify quality standards. Otis Elevator promises equipment repair within 2 hours, 24 hours a day, 7 days a week. A phone call is all it takes to mobilize Otis. The quality of service in the elevator business is expressed in terms of speed, acceleration, deceleration, stopping, sound, and light level. American Express has defined two standards for its credit card: a 24 hour response to the credit request and zero defect on the card itself. Club Med has defined precise quality service standards for the behavior of its Gracious Organizers (GOs). It uses words such as courtesy, imagination, kindness, attention, and generosity. These standards are used in recruiting as well as in training. Sovran Bank has standards for answering requests for credit, which include not only the financial criteria, but also style and tone of the response. A standard need not be absolute to be effective. It must simply express a commitment with regard to the promise made to the customer. For example, American Airlines defined a standard for baggage losses: fewer than 1200 per month. Sound arbitrary or extremely liberal? Not at all. Its closest competitor loses nearly 1300.

Service Quality Standards Must be Understood and Applied Throughout the Organization

Service quality standards must be operational throughout an organization. Lufthansa makes this statement in its service promise: "Businessmen want to get where they're going, not wait." Converted into standards, the message to management becomes: "The passenger must not wait more than 30 minutes at each step of a trip." Management must consider all of the elements that might affect the length of a stop-over: flight schedules, flight time, baggage check-in, baggage claim services, and so on. Every employee in the baggage handling department, for instance, is guided by the same standard whether the employee checks the suitcases, unloads them, or drives the baggage tractor. (See Figure 11.)

The closer the standard gets to the person who actually serves the public the more its components must be broken down into specific requirements. This practice will ensure the fullest customer satisfaction.

General standard	Specific standards						
Company promise (general standard of service quality)	Quality standards for luggage service			Quality standards for the luggage handler			
	Tasks to be accomplished	How (method)	Result for the customer	Tasks to be accomplished	How (method)	Result for the customer	
The passengers will have their luggage delivered to the pick-up point in less than fifteen minutes	Position the carts x minutes before the arrival Unload the containers in order	Obtain flight information	Passengers are able to pick up their luggage in less than fifteen minutes	Place the cart as close as possible to the conveyor belt	Approach from the front	Passengers can pick up their luggage in less than fifteen minutes	

Figure 11. Service Quality Standards

Every employee has to understand how his or her specific job contributes to creating a better service.

In a typical scenario there will be +/–50 service quality standards for general management and +/–1000 for the departments that contribute directly to service quality. These standards constitute the backbone of the company's service quality. They are also a good indication of the company's service know-how. The standards are also useful for training programs. The result expected by the customer is often omitted

iars that prefer to concentrate on operations (e.g., set a table, repair a machine, prepare a stage).

Comprehensive understanding of the standards can contribute to employee morale. Employees who understand the importance of their specific jobs will generally take pride in doing them better.

Train Personnel About Quality Standards

Standards must be communicated. They must be disseminated throughout the company. There are two ways to do this: training and coaching.

British Airways organized a three-day course to disseminate the details of its new service quality standards. The program reached each of the airline's 30,000 employees. Club Med created six-day seminars to similarly inform its 2,000 village managers. The process took eight months, as each seminar was limited to 50 people. Singapore Airlines insists on 12 weeks of training before a flight attendant meets her first customer.

Coaching has made many restaurant and hotel companies more successful. A department manager demonstrates a procedure. He monitors the employee while the latter performs the same procedure. Errors are corrected on the spot. The coach must have excellent communication and demonstration skills and he must have the time to devote to the trainee.

Investment in training will pay long-range dividends by ensuring compliance with quality standards. Although classroom training is less risky than on-the-job training, the effective trainer never forgets the maxim that a person remembers

- 10% of what she reads
- 20% of what she hears
- 30% of what she sees

- 50% of what she hears and sees
- 70% of what she says and does
- 90% of what is explained while it is being done

Some people are born with a sense of service. The less fortunate have to work to acquire one. The competitive CEO should know how much the company is investing annually to train telephone operators, delivery drivers, receptionists, and counter clerks in comparison with the amount invested in training bookkeepers. The CEO should also know much time is devoted to making certain that the quality standards are clear and understandable.

Delivering a Customer-Oriented Service

Once the service quality standards are specified, the process of defining the relevant components begins. Four elements come into play:

- the people who provide the service
- the equipment and machines that accompany the service
- the procedures and methods to be followed to furnish the service
- the raw materials used in the service

A department store may decide to develop a competitive edge based on welcome, comfort and convenience, and freedom of choice. It will have to study flow patterns and interior decor (equipment), provide a large variety of brands (raw materials), design methods for welcoming and informing the customer and for managing inventory (procedures and methods), and select and retrain sales staff, cashiers, reception, and information personnel (the people).

A broad smile will not be enough to ensure a competitive advantage. Nor will pretty paint. The entire organization must be redesigned to address the service goal. The standard is only the starting point. Quality does not tolerate approximation. Every detail must be considered. Management of a service quality policy can be a very complex process. The receptionist's smile, broad though it may be, will never be able to compensate for an overloaded telephone system. Incidentally, implementation problems are *not* the customer's problem. He or she couldn't care less if delivery times are not respected because the widget factory is on strike.

But management can develop a set of procedures to deal with a late widget problem. The first step should stress honesty. The customer should be told why an order is delayed and why the company is proposing an alternate supplier. Second, a responsible person should be assigned to manage the transaction. This person should personally take the unfilled order in hand and try to get it filled. If an alternate source of supply cannot be located, the customer should either be reimbursed for any prepaid charges or offered an alternative solution. (The alternative solution should be considered even if it would involve a loss on the sale.) If all else fails, the complaint manager might want to consider parting with a part of her personal collection of widgets. The customer will be impressed with the extraordinary effort expended on his behalf. He will probably be a customer for a long time to come. If, however, there is no alternative solution, any explanation may be insufficient. The customer may be dissatisfied. A dissatisfied service customer may be an ex-customer.

In order to monitor quality at the moment of service, it is necessary to list the various steps through which the customer passes to acquire the service. At each step, customer expectations must be defined and converted into quality standards. The error possibilities of each step must be identified and compared to the resources available to prevent repetition. (See Figure 12.)

Steps through which the customer passes	→	→	→	→
What can go wrong?	?	?	?	?
Ways and means • people • methods • equipment • materials				

Figure 12. The Analysis of Quality

This method will probably surprise companies who concentrate on their navel rather than on their customer. They will discover that service orientation consists of asking the customer:

- what is his credit problem before the name of his father and his mother
- what she wants to buy before her payment conditions
- where she hurts before her insurance policy number
- whether she has an urgent job before her address and telephone

The method is equally valid for organizing leisure activities as it is for delivering mail. Federal Express developed a letter delivery system that ensures its service quality. Each piece of mail passes through a series of operations on its way to final delivery. An error could occur during any of the operations. But the Fed Ex system anticipates errors and provides each handler with the resources to correct them on the spot.

American Hospital Supply designed a computer program to provide its customer with a user-friendly and efficient order system. (It typically costs a hospital about $100 to place an order. These costs are mainly administrative and do not include storage costs that are difficult to measure since many articles are immediately dispersed throughout the various departments.) Thanks to continuous computer-to-computer contact, hospitals can now place several orders per day, at minimal cost. Excessive paperwork and large inventories are no longer necessary. Everything is recorded in the American Hospital Supply data base. Hospital administration accesses the AHS data base to find out how many operating room masks it has on hand. An innovative application of a commonplace technology has provided AHS with a competitive service edge. The shared screen technique monitors the customer's inventory and provides it with an efficient, easy to use order system at the same time.

Today, computers can be used to record the volume of calls received or put on hold and the average number of rings per call. With a bit of ingenuity, quality management is possible!

Motivate Personnel—A Convinced Employee is a Convinced Customer

Effective internal communications can serve multiple purposes. They can be used to inform employees about quality standards and about the company's promise to the customer. The employee can gain a better understanding of how his or her contribution fits into the bigger picture. Communication can also stimulate pride and mobilize enthusiasm. Many service oriented firms create advertising campaigns starring company personnel. They make the employees TV stars.

Why not? Service is a people business. When the customer is served by the person he or she recognizes from a TV commercial, the customer's impressed at being served by a television personality. Likewise, the employee is impressed with his or her newfound status. A few years ago, to conclude a company quality improvement program, British Airways introduced a new poster, picturing its stewards as Supermen. Nevertheless, there are companies that refuse to spotlight their employees. They are wrong.

To sell the customer on its service quality, a company must first sell its employees. A skeptical employee will not convince a customer. The best companies launch full-fledged internal campaigns to sell their personnel on the desired level of excellence. These campaigns not only ensure an indispensable continuity in communication, but also have the effect of stimulating pride and morale.

A successful campaign must begin with a clear, "catchy" slogan. The slogan must capture the essence of the campaign. The company must organize a series of events that reinforce good service behavior. Complimentary letters from managers, articles in the company newsletter, regular quality meetings, awards that honor initiatives, contests for the best welcome of the month, or the best repair job, election of a "service champion" are just a few ideas. *Personnel must be made to understand the importance of quality.*

SAS, the Swedish airline, was losing $70 million a year before Jan Carlzon took over as CEO. Fifteen months later, it broke all profit records. Carlzon does not attribute the recovery to his clairvoyance. He understood that the destiny of SAS was not in his hands, but in those of its 20 thousand employees. He met with them all to tell them: "From now on, SAS is the business traveler's European airline. Here are the general guidelines of this policy. Now it is up to you."

THREE EXAMPLES OF QUALITY ANALYSIS

Example 1: The Sailboard at Club Med

Service strategy: freedom of choice to quickly take advantage of the village.

Service quality standards: continuous "self service" sports activities from 9 AM to 5 PM with a course from 9 AM to 11 AM and from 2 PM to 4 PM for those wishing to participate; security assured; availability of a board within 15 minutes; use of the board for at least one hour.

Service delivery system: a welcome; boards and accessories available; a lifeguard boat; information about weather conditions and any dangers (rocks, currents, sea conditions).

Quality analysis:

1. What are the steps through which the customer passes with the corresponding service standards?

The Gracious Member (GM) goes to the location activity	The GM is welcomed (by someone)	The GM takes a sailboard (within 15 minutes)	The GM uses the sailboard (minimum 1 hour)	The GM gives back the sailboard	The GM leaves

2. What is it that can make each step go wrong?

• Complicated schedules • Location poorly indicated • Location difficult to get to	• No welcome • Cold and unpleasant welcome • No information about the dangers • No recommendations about the type of sailboard to use	• No board • Board in poor condition • It is decided that the GM cannot leave without a lesson • The GM cannot carry the board alone	• Equipment broken • Board sinks • The GM cannot come back alone • The GM gets sunburnt	• The GM must return the board before the hour is over • The GM cannot carry it alone • The GM must clean it • The GM dismantles it and someone takes it • The GM returns far from the starting point and must carry it	• Possession lost • No goodbye

3. To ensure quality, what are the resources in terms of methods, people, materials, and equipment?

People	• Number of Gracious Organizers (GO) • Training of GOs	• Assistance	• Safety	• Assistance	• Courtesy • Safety
Material • Posting of panels • Direction panels • Orientation panels			• Lifeguard boat • Sun screen cream		
Equipment • Pathways cleared		• No extra equipment		• Better boards • More boards	• Safety
Methods • Schedule planning	• Finding information and communication of information	• Interview • Choice of material	• Choice of material	• Sailboard maintenance • Test/evaluation of experience	

Example 2: The Federal Express Service

Service strategy: deliver company mail within 24 hours or 48 hours to any place in the world.

Service quality standards: delivery within 24 hours; without errors; without damage (safety); accessible during office hours.

Service delivery system: collection points easily accessible to the customer; dispatching (sorting, sending); an arrival collection point.

Quality analysis:

1. The steps

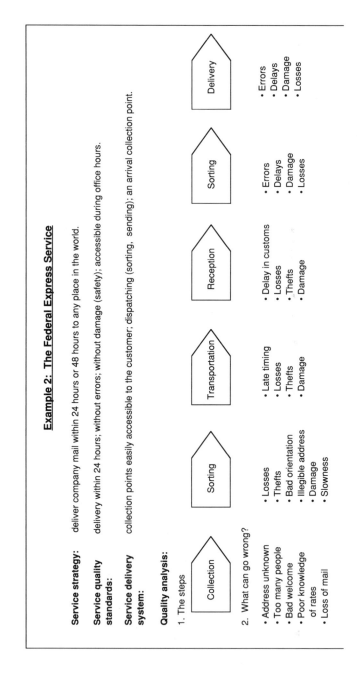

Collection	Sorting	Transportation	Reception	Sorting	Delivery

2. What can go wrong?

Collection
- Address unknown
- Too many people
- Bad welcome
- Poor knowledge of rates
- Loss of mail

Sorting
- Losses
- Thefts
- Bad orientation
- Illegible address
- Damage
- Slowness

Transportation
- Late timing
- Losses
- Thefts
- Damage

Reception
- Delay in customs
- Losses
- Thefts
- Damage

Sorting
- Errors
- Delays
- Damage
- Losses

Delivery
- Errors
- Delays
- Damage
- Losses

3. The resources

People
• More personnel trained for receiving customers

Equipment
• Location of shops

Material

Methods/procedures
• Procedure followed
• Scheduling based upon activity

• Training for sorting

• Automation of sorting/ distribution

• Sorting method
• Protection
• Identification of letters

• Choice of transportation companies

• Containers

• Negotiations with airlines
• Insurance

• Negotiation with customs

Example 3: Microcomputer Sales

Service strategy: give customers the best availability in the whole industry.

Quality standards: repair service 5 days out of 7, 10 hours per day, on the dealer's premises; if the breakdown is not found after one hour, call the manager if, at the end of six hours, the computer is not repaired, the ongoing work is taken over by another computer or another computer is lent.

Quality analysis:

1. The steps

| Telephone | Bring the micro-computer to the dealer | The computer is repaired | It is given back |

2. What can go wrong?

• No answer	• Does not know the details of the repair	• No parts available	• It doesn't work
• Not friendly, not personalized	• Cannot give an idea of price	• Does not succeed in identifying the cause	• No explanation why repair is impossible
• Not routed to the right person	• Does not ask the right questions to find the cause	• Not enough people for the repair	• Exorbitant invoice
• Telephone busy	• Bad welcome		• Erroneous invoice
• Poor knowledge of the particular model			• Customer not notified when the computer is repaired

3. The ways and means

People	• Training repairman for receiving customers	• Training in diagnosis, welcome, preparing invoice	• Training	
Equipment	• Telephone switchboard		• Machines available • Spare parts	• Loan of machines
Materials	• Documentation to be clarified			
Methods	• Methods for routing the customer	• Information about time necessary • Know-how	• Methods for diagnosis, monitoring and scheduling the repair	• Invoicing • Inspection and testing • Notifying customer

In order to ease the pains associated with its recent merger with Piedmont Airlines, USAir instituted an employee information hot line. Employees can call it from anywhere in the world. A series of trunk dialings provide information on health benefits, new flight destinations, or the latest news about the company, its plans, and its accomplishments. This is an excellent way to reaffirm the company credo!

Piedmont Airlines used to present graduate flight attendants with a company license plate. In addition to promoting morale, the plate provided easy access to the company parking lot. But the idea hit a snag. Some states demand that every car carry the state license on both the front and rear bumpers. USAir solved the snag. It sent a company plate to each employee in states requiring only one plate. Employees in states demanding two plates received a license plate frame bearing the company logo in large red and blue letters.

This chapter should leave the reader with one unimpeachable conclusion: A service orientation adopted throughout a delivery system can be a source of significant savings.

Self-diagnosis

- Do you have service quality standards?
- How many?
- Are they expressed in terms of results for the customer?
- Do they include tasks and the method for getting these results?
- Are they suitable in their formulation and their scope for each level of personnel?
- Does everybody know them?
- Are they measurable?
- Do they correspond to your promise, to your service strategy?

- In your training programs, before teaching the tasks to be performed and the methods, is everyone reminded how this serves the customer?
- Is your service delivery system customer oriented? Or is it more oriented to the inside of the company?
- Are your employees convinced of the service quality of your company? Have you tried to convince them? With the same care and effort that you give to your external communications?

CHAPTER SEVEN

———

The Hunt for Errors,
The Quest for Zero Defect

QUALITY defects never es-
cape customer scrutiny. In a
service industry, zero defect is not a luxury. It is a necessity.
The idea of zero defect must be studied in relation to the level
of service and the quality standards identified by the company. Zero defect is a relative concept. When American
Airlines loses fewer than 1200 pieces of luggage items per
month, the quality standard that it has set for itself, it reaches
zero defect. Its closest competitor loses nearly 1300 pieces.
American should not expect a zero loss rate. The cost would
be prohibitive. A standard with a zero luggage loss rate
would only become necessary if, due to word of mouth, the
cost of passenger desertion became greater than the cost of
indemnification.

"Do it right the first time." This is the surest way to reach
zero defect in service quality. It is impossible to erase an
error once the service has been rendered.

Do it Right the First Time

Doing it right the first time is a matter of attitude. Employees who will most readily adopt the idea are those who:

91

- like what they're doing. (It is very difficult, if not impossible, to expect someone to do something right the first time if he or she doesn't feel comfortable with the job. The nature of the work is also important. It helps if complexity and gratification factors of the job correspond to worker expectations.)
- have pride in their work. (Pride is a major consideration for every person in direct contact with the customer.)

Granada Motorways Services, a British service station chain, increased its sales by 25 percent by practicing "do it right the first time" in their restrooms. Each restroom attendant was issued an attractive, new uniform, a chair, and a table. Each was trained to warmly welcome customers with a personalized touch. The restrooms were rearranged to include a spacious coatroom and clean premises. Results? Customers spend more time (and money) in the station.

At the Bermuda Onion, a fashionable Paris restaurant, the waitresses's changing rooms are designed like movie star dressing rooms, complete with costume wardrobes, individual make-up tables, mirrors, neon lighting, and stage settings. The Bermuda Onion waitresses feel like movie stars. They welcome like stars and they serve like stars.

Pride is not only a question of ethics. It also results from how a person thinks he or she is perceived by peers. Many factors can increase staff pride and therefore its willingness to do it right the first time: uniforms, badges, internal communications, a review process, the stature given to relationships with customers, the manner in which the staff is addressed.

A Total Commitment to One's Work

Zero defect requires discipline and a total commitment to one's work. The rate of absenteeism in Japan is 3 percent. In Great Britain it's 15 percent.

Singapore Airlines recruits 300 flight attendants every year. It's training program is 12 weeks long. Tardy arrival at three training sessions disqualifies a candidate. Message sent, message received!

Enthusiasm

Finally, zero defect is a question of enthusiasm. A recent study showed that enthusiastic people have the following characteristics:

- they are sensitive to compliments from the customer and are motivated by such compliments
- they feel that the company is providing support and allowing freedom to take initiatives in the field

The individual's sensitivity to compliments can be identified at the time of recruitment and nourished by the company. Management has only to facilitate letters of congratulations from customers and pass them on to the responsible party. It might be possible to extend the interaction time between the contact personnel and customers, giving the customer time to express satisfaction. For example, on short flights, an airline might limit its services in order to give the crew time to chat with the passengers and for the passengers to compliment them.

To select enthusiastic contact personnel, many companies have developed tests subjecting the candidates to real working situations. A video shows a customer in a hurry. He wants to be served before the others. Candidates responses are observed. Test situations should be similar to those that actually occur frequently, and they should be designed to identify enthusiastic behavior. It's equally important for management to make certain that employees who have already proven themselves are not slighted in the process.

USAir issues future flight attendants a series of manuals that specify the nature of the work, the quality levels demanded, and all service procedures. There will be a quiz tomorrow morning! Some candidates are intimidated by the thickness of the manuals and resign from the program. The losses are easily offset by the guarantee of quality delivered by those who overcome this initial stumbling block.

Contact personnel also need to feel that their decisions will be supported by management. When they feel secure, the results can be astonishing.

A village manager at Club Med had prepared, according to custom, a Christmas Eve celebration. Also, according to custom, he invited local civic leaders. The locals arrived in greater numbers than expected. It was soon apparent that there was not going to be enough food. The village manager asked the Gracious Members to join him in welcoming the guests. For their trouble and for the unexpected problems, a second Christmas dinner would be served to them the following day. Favorably impressed, many Gracious Members returned to the village for repeat visits. That meant more business.

The village manager's initiative would not have been possible if he thought it would be censured.

In a recent British Airways survey, passengers identified the two service criteria that they considered most important when traveling abroad. First, flexibility. Passengers wanted to know that the airline would help them organize alternate travel solutions in case of problems. Next, passengers were concerned about compensation, that is, the manner in which they would be indemnified for inconvenience due to company error.

It is essential that a company delegate certain prerogatives to the contact personnel to enable them to take initiatives and to rectify any situation that deviates from service quality standards. Agents, reception personnel, delivery people, technicians, hotel managers, and customer representatives serve in the front lines. They must know what initiatives they can take on their own. Having front-line personnel list the initiative they can take without or only with prior authorization may be revealing. If they have to seek approval too often they may not have the tools to properly serve their customers. Without flexibility, contact staff can only respond with evasive answers. Evasive answers mean frustrated customers.

Doing it right the first time may require an investment in recruitment, selection, training and stimulation of personnel. But the cost should not be a prohibiting factor. Lack of quality is more expensive.

A firm needed reception personnel to work at various European sites. The task involved several steps: recruitment of candidates, analysis of dossiers, preselection, interviews, final selection, assignment of the candidate, and acceptance by the person responsible at the site.

As standard practice, the firm studied resumes submitted in response to a newspaper ad. They selected candidates for interviews. Immediately after the interviews, the best applicants were sent directly to the job site. Result? Twenty percent resigned before the end of the first month. Amount wasted: $800,000.

Three departments shared the responsibility for the loss; recruitment, personnel and site management. The $800,000 wasn't the only loss. Most of the 20 percent who resigned performed poorly while on the job. The newcomers were not prepared for their duties. They grew angry with the firm and, as often happens, passed their anger on to the customers.

The attrition could have been avoided. First, the firm could have defined the recruitment criteria. The initial screening would have been standardized. A basic, service oriented test would have enabled more rigorous preselection.

Interviewers should have known more about the nature of the work and the skills required. Site managers should have been made part of the final selection process. A welcome booklet would have informed the newcomers about job requirements and behavior standards. The new employees could have been assigned to a training program.

Had *all* of these alternatives been instituted, the cost would still have been far less than $800,000. Doing it right the first time may not be cost free, but it is always cheaper than sub-par work.

Zero Defect Entails An Uncompromising Error Chase

Track Down and Chase Errors

The error chase consists of tracking down, classifying, analyzing, and correcting all the deviations from quality standards. Before the chase begins, two points demand attention. First, the error chase should not become a witch hunt. The discovery of a conformity deviation should end in corrective action, not in blame. Employees will not participate in an error chase if they think they will be punished for the anomalies. Next, the error chase must include everyone who has contact with the customer. Don't call in the FBI. The error chase must be perceived as a constructive management approach.

An error chase should include all the service elements, methods, procedures, equipment, and tasks that do not meet the quality promise. The error chase should be spontaneous and informal. There should be no need to establish a quality circle to pick up a scrap of paper on a hotel lobby floor. That's everybody's job. Picking up papers is not the exclusive domain of the cleaning personnel. When the telephone rings, everyone should feel concerned. The person nearest the phone should answer. No need to wait for the receptionist to come back from lunch.

In some cases, the error chase involves major, more complex problems requiring substantial modifications to company procedures. An investment may be involved. Several company departments may be affected by the change. In such cases, a formal error chasing procedure must be established.

Organizing the Error Chase

Most error chases are initiated by a working group whose first assignment is to identify, list, and classify errors. The next step involves a search for solutions based on available resources. Information traffic is organized vertically from bottom to top to propose solutions and from top to bottom, to approve suggested improvements.

The working groups may take three different forms: quality project teams, quality action squads, or quality circles. Each group will have different types of assignments. If an error is located in a detail of furnishing service, it requires immediate and simple solutions, and more contact personnel need to be included.

The quality circle will only be effective if management offers highly visible support. It's helpful if the idea of participation already exists in the firm's management structure. The circle concept will not work effectively if the company maintains an authoritarian posture in some matters and encourages participation in others.

It is also important that the circle leader be comfortable with his or her function, both in relation to management and to the group members. This person will benefit from training in active listening and group dynamics.

Timely reward and recognition for tangible results will always improve the success of a quality circle. The circle leader should start the group with problems that are relatively simple to solve, and then publish the results in the house journal. It goes without saying that the group must receive the backing and support of management. (The more the problems to be addressed affect the bottom line, the more management will want to be involved.) Management also has the responsibility of defining the quality standards that the circle will address, as well as the scope of the error chase. At Club Med, the error chase program began only after management approved the quality standards and set them down in a 1200-page book.

Error Chase: Everyone's Obsession, Every Instant

In an interview with International Management Magazine, the CEO of the Movenpick hotel chain pointed out that it's a mistake to think that service quality and customer satisfaction are ever definitively acquired. The process is an on-going one. In the frequent two-day meetings that he organizes with his staff, detailed matters dealing with the clarity of the instructions to be followed in case of theft or fire, new coat hangers, and guests' jogging cards are often discussed. He sends fictitious application letters to the personnel department to study the speed and quality of the responses. Several times a year, he checks with guests to test the quality of the hotel service.

Suggestions Moving Up and Responses Moving Down:
The Role of the Quality Manager

The working group needs a system to facilitate the communication of employee suggestions and the decisions taken by management. Many companies appoint a quality manager to manage this traffic. Others have formed quality committees. The advantage of the latter is that management can participate in the process from the beginning. The committee examines proposals and passes them on to the quality manager for follow-up.

Quality managers are facilitators. They report to management and manage correspondents in the various units, divisions, departments,or sections of the organization. Their responsibilities are many.

They must facilitate the quality improvement process. They will assist operational people in the formulation of quality standards and try to get the concurrence of general management to agree they will facilitate the distribution of the standards throughout the organization.

Quality managers may be called upon to design a format in which the standards can be written, then edit them and create dissemination methods. At the request of general management, they may help the working groups with planning. Finally, they will participate in cost assessment and help identify the benefits of the solutions.

Quality managers must represent the customer's point of view. They design and conduct customer satisfaction surveys and distribute the results within the company. By emphasizing the results of the survey, they help the departments define service delivery standards. The quality manager represents the customer's point of view in all management meetings. He or she manages inquiries into specific points of service.

Quality managers perform quality audits. In the audit function, the quality manager acts neither as an inspector nor as a police officer. The audits are run in close coordination with department managers; the quality manager summarizes the results with the department managers and then communicates them to general management.

Quality managers prepare the service quality training tools and manage training programs.

They are quality advocates. They stimulate the spirit of quality, everyday and everywhere. They encourages innovation. They circulate articles, personal reports, and results within

QUALITY MGR =
CORPORATE TRAINING/
AUDITOR

the company. They test competitive services and communicate the results. They record internal innovations, create contests, and choose quality winners. Quality managers guide innovative projects during their preliminary phases and propose progress producing projects to management.

Quality managers are the company's quality representative to the outside world. They join trade associations, participate in conferences, give speeches and grant interviews concerning the company's experience in the service quality field.

The quality manager has no formal authority. He or she must rely on influence and persuasion. In order to be credible, quality managers must prove that they deserve to be considered mentor, respected for their contributions, and they must act with the unconditional support of management.

The quality manager must create a network of correspondents within the company, in order to collect relevant data. These correspondents may help to prepare the error chase training tools.

No need to set up a quality management bureaucracy. One full-time person can do the job. He or she can establish an informal network of contacts and correspondents to assure input from all relevant departments. That's all. At IBM-France, for example, the team responsible for quality management comprises a manager and three assistants.

The Error Chase and Time

To sustain motivation and enthusiasm in the error chase, it is imperative that the ideas that come to management receive immediate attention and quick response. Receipt of each idea should be acknowledged within 48 hours and a response should be returned within 30 days. In some companies, 300 to 1,000 recommendations may be handled each year.

One way of ensuring speedy action is to allocate operational management a small budget that they can use to finance quality projects. Formal steps and procedures can be bypassed. The truly innovative idea may not wait until next year!

An Error Chase Will Include:

- the error targeted
- an analysis of the causes
- a list of possible solutions
- a detailed explanation of the recommended solution
- results of experimentation (if the solution needs to be tested)
- the present total cost resulting from lack of quality
- the total cost at zero defect
- the expected investment
- the consequences for other parts of the company
- the projected time for the project to become profitable

The Error Chase Begins with Customer Service

To achieve consistent quality, it is essential to examine the company's internal services, as well as the services provided to the customer. Many companies linger over the former to the detriment of the latter. Internal services must be evaluated in light of their contributions to outside services. They cannot be ends in themselves. Any error chase begins with the customer. Customer expectations should define the demands that departments make on each other.

In the 1960s, many companies suffered from a "dialogue of the deaf" with centralized computer departments whose functions related more to bookkeeping than to management. It often required a great deal of shouting, with proof in hand that customer-based demands were not being met before data processing supervisors would choose to be responsive. Customer expectations, however, will eventually produce agreement between sales and production managements, between research scientists and treasurers, between financial controllers and division managers.

Front-line employees receive a genuine stimulus when the process begins by studying customer satisfaction. They will be better motivated if their efforts result in increased sales than if they are merely thanked for being nice to the other departments.

Managers should reread procedure manuals and interdepartmental documents to make certain that they all address the needs of the customers. Many will be surprised at the number of procedures, documents, and rules that never mention the customer.

The Tools for the Error Chase

Industry has already designed tools to improve product quality. With minor adaptations, many of these tools can be used in the search for service quality. An error chase has two phases: identifying errors and seeking causes. Some industry tools can be applied at each phase.

Identifying Errors

Some industry tools can be used to detect and classify errors. Brainstorming sessions, suggestion boxes, complaint letter analysis, qualifying reimbursements by cause, and user surveys are a few examples.

The errors must be classified and prioritized. The best known method for establishing a hierarchy of errors is the Pareto analysis. Each error is assigned a coefficient indicating its magnitude. The quality group will tackle the weightiest errors first.

The relative weight of errors is defined using criteria similar to those employed in manufacturing. Instead of calculating the frequency of rejects during production or counting the number of pieces that do not pass inspection, for example, a service program will calculate the frequency of late deliveries, the frequency of repairs and reimbursements, the number of telephone rings per call, the number of files mislaid.

Many services do not lend themselves to measurement. One cannot measure the frequency of a smile. Some managers prefer to use a point system. Starting with a predetermined number of points, say 100, group members are asked to list errors and assign point values. The total of the values cannot exceed 100.

Group members must agree on the criteria by which errors will be classified. Frequency is not always a valid indicator. It's equally important to avoid reasoning by averages. Market sectors must be clearly identified since different sectors may have different expectations. The advertiser who devotes two million dollars to an advertising campaign does not have the same expectations as the one who spends $200,000. The customer who buys 30 computers does not have the same requirements as the customer who buys 3. When listing errors, weight must be modified accordingly.

Seeking Causes

Causes must be identified before solutions can be defined. They can be tracked down by utilizing the Ishikawa diagram, the "herringbone" analysis. Causes can be identified by sampling the service. This is a particularly effective approach when the service is rendered at several locations. The solution process begins by systematically modifying one variable at a time. Such a trial makes it possible to test the situation before adopting a definitive solution.

Each has built-in advantages and disadvantages. But each tool must be used systematically. Being systematic avoids discussions in a vacuum, unfounded disagreements, and lost time. Participants must understand the importance of the process and not see it as a theoretical exercise. The goal is to provide satisfaction to customers!

Self-diagnosis

- Do your service people like what they are doing? Are they proud? Are they enthusiastic?
- What have you done in terms of selection, training, motivation to make them proud of their work?
- How much independent authority is granted to employees in contact with the customer? What can't they to do?
- Do you have tests for selecting those enthusiastic about providing service?
- Do your employees ever receive letters of praise?
- Do you have an organized error chase procedure?
- If it has already started, is your quality program more oriented toward external quality or internal quality?

CHAPTER EIGHT

Measuring Customer Satisfaction

*T*HE CUSTOMER'S perception of the quality of a service is often different from the perception of the provider. The difference results from a number of factors. First, there may be a misunderstanding about the criterion applied. A consulting firm recently organized a seminar. The organizer had been assured that the participants would enjoy the best of service during the coffee break, that is, porcelain dishes and real silverware, tablecloths, cookies and crackers, coffee and tea, costumed waiters with many platters and many smiles. Quite sure of himself, the organizer later asked the participants to judge the service quality of the coffee break. He was stupefied to learn that 80 percent of the participants were dissatisfied. He didn't understand that the executives, during break time, wanted telephones and bathrooms.

A company can also become the prisoner of its own language. House jargon is often used to measure the quality of the service offered, but it may be unsuitable to measure the quality of service purchased. For example:

The firm conceives the measure:	The customer perceives the measure:
The breadth of range	The extent of the choice and the counsel
The fittings of the display	The presence of merchandise
Credit card acceptance	Spontaneous gifts
The architecture	Comfort and convenience
The premium conditions	The advantages of the insurance payment schedules

A company's obsession with internal organization can constitute another substantial distortion. It is a rare company that places itself in the customer's shoes when measuring satisfaction. Some companies even consider customers a nuisance. What savings could be made if *they* were not there! Unfortunately, without *them*, there would be no company.

Finally, a company may believe that its service is so unique that there is no basis for comparison. This company *assumes* that the customer will be satisfied. After all, if the company is the world's only producer of left-handed widgets, why should it worry about customer satisfaction? The fallacy: Customers may find ways to adapt right-handed widgets or build their products without using any widgets at all.

Consumer surveys can be revealing. In one such survey published in 1986 in "50 Millions de Consommateurs" (the French consumer report), consumers were asked to rate the services of national utilities against private sector firms. The National Electricity Company received an 82 percent satisfaction rating, followed by the National Telephone Company with 80 percent, the National Railroad and the

National Post Office, each with 75 percent. Hospitals, whose services require considerably more interaction for longer periods, received a rating of 53 percent. McDonald's scored a flashy 95 percent.

TARP data suggests that an alarm should go off when satisfaction rates fall below 80 percent. A durable competitive advantage requires an average of at least 94 percent.

Satisfaction Surveys

There is a simple way to learn about customer satisfaction. Ask customers about their feelings, ask them regularly, track the changes, and measure the progress. A successful survey begins with a good questionnaire. But a good questionnaire is not built from the inside out. An effective one will optimally gauge the customer's feelings. There's no value in asking questions about matters that don't concern the customer or about which the customer has never reflected. Hence, to build an effective questionnaire, it is indispensable to begin with a qualitative phase.

Individual or group interviews will give one a clue to the customer's concerns, expectations and language. A strong data base will include information gathered from former, current, and potential customers. The questions that are based on interviews, will then focus on the various aspects of quality that are important to the buyer.

Individual survey results are not very illuminating. Once results are collected, they must be compared with the results of the competition or, if that is not possible, with the quality perceived for an analogous service. An 80 percent satisfaction rate is less acceptable when management learns that the competition rates 90 percent. It goes without saying that a difference favoring the competitor demands a more energetic response than would a slight drop in satisfaction.

ın measurements may be taken daily, weekly, monthly, or annually. Everything depends upon purchase frequency and the speed with which the company can modify its quality program. Club Med checks the satisfaction of its Gracious Members every week. It is able to rectify oversights immediately. Swissair performs monthly samplings. The results of the survey are submitted to the chairman of the board. A typical survey question asks: "Did you have to wait more than or less than three minutes at check-in?" The questionnaire is given to randomly selected passengers, in an envelope upon which is written: "The better we know your opinion, the better we can serve you." This questionnaire, filled in with some 5,000 quality comments, is analyzed every three months, and the results are compared to the quality measured in the field by the supervisor at each airport. Xerox conducts annual surveys that, among other items, monitor after-sale service. The data are compared to the results of surveys the company automatically performs three months after an installation.

The renewal of a maintenance or insurance contract, the periodic statement from a building manager, bank, or credit card company, a follow-up letter, all present opportunities to include a customer satisfaction survey. Cost need not be a prohibiting factor.

The skeptic may observe: "Only unhappy customers answer" or "That will just bother the customer" or "The questionnaire will give the customer bad ideas." It has never been demonstrated that a questionnaire unfavorably influenced a customer. It is more probable that some degree of dissatisfaction pre-dated the questionnaire. People seldom feel harassed when they feel they're contributing to research that will directly benefit them.

The survey must result in tangible action. A stack of questionnaires is only a pile of paper. Merely counting them is not enough. They must be studied in detail before they can return on investment. Once the survey results are collated, they must be analyzed. How does management know whether 20 percent unsatisfied customers means 20 percent lost customers or whether only a proportion of them have deserted the firm? How many of the 20 percent dissatisfied customers will also speak badly of the company? To answer this type of question, buying behavior must be examined and the effect of word of mouth measured. Only then can management begin to draw informed conclusions. Research has shown that among the dissatisfied, there are always about 15 percent who would have been impossible to satisfy under any circumstances. If the total dissatisfaction rate is 20 percent, this means that only 3 percent (15% of 20% = 3%) of the client base is irretrievably lost. Finally, management may choose to identify a number of faithful customers. Interviews with faithful customers will provide data vital to analyzing the attitude of the dissatisfieds.

Complaint Letters: A Source of Profit

Surveys are not the only means by which to measure customer satisfaction. Complaint or compliment letters can also become quality management tools. Although complaint and compliment letters add a touch of detail that no survey can cover, they do not provide a basis for sound statistical analysis.

Few people take the trouble to write. Understandably, unhappy customers comprise the larger percentage of the letter writers. Dissatisfied people tend to write more often than satisfied people. A company can expect to receive 10 complaint letters for each compliment letter.

The TARP study found only 4 percent of dissatisfied customers write letters of complaint. Though it must be carefully managed, the complaint letter can be a powerful tool. Between 55 percent and 70 percent of complaining customers will use a service again if they are answered quickly. The rate climbs to 95 percent, if they are answered *quickly* and *well*. A quick response must be made in less than two weeks, preceded by an acknowledgement within 48 hours. Add it up! If a company receives 1,000 letters per year and if they're answered quickly and well, 950 customers can be recovered. If each customer spends $1000 a year, sales will increase by $100,000. It should take no more than one-fourth of a person/year to answer the 1000 letters, and the correspondent could easily become the most productive person in the company!

To recover 95 percent of the unsatisfied customers, it is important, first of all, that the letters be properly processed. A lost letter is definitely worse than no letter at all. There is a very simple way to make certain that complaint letters receive proper attention; tell customers *where* and *to whom* to write. Include the information on all of the documents that leave the company, including invoices, monthly statements, packaging, advertising circulars, and so on. The best way to increase the number of letters is to have them sent to The Boss. It's also an excellent way for The Boss to remain in contact with the customers.

Imagine the following message at the bottom of a credit card statement:

"If you are not satisfied, write to me. I will answer you."

> Signed,
> "The Boss"

A bad answer to a letter of complaint will include the following mistakes:

Date: (very long after receipt of the complaint— 15 days to 3 months)

Dear Sir: (You have to keep your distance with a nuisance.)

Ist paragraph: You may be right but I am still surprised because . . . (you're too demanding, this doesn't usually happen and I don't really believe it happened to you).

2nd paragraph: Be assured that the responsible personnel will be punished . . . (hopefully you'll feel guilty and end this correspondence in its tracks. You don't really like people to be punished, do you?).

3rd paragraph: Anyway, I trust this won't effect our relationship (we're not really so bad, after all).

4th paragraph: I think I answered all your questions and I thank you for bringing the problem to my attention . . . (don't bother me any more with this trivia. Do you think I don't know how to run this business?).

Signature,

(A secretary signing for Mr. X)

(The answer is from Mr. X. The complaint wasn't even addressed to him. That really makes you feel important.)

The good answer will include the following elements:

Date: (under 48 hours)

Dear Client: (You're very important to us!)

Ist paragraph: Thanks for taking the time to write . . . (After all, you didn't have to. You could have switched to the competition and never bothered to tell me.)

2nd paragraph: You're right! We don't have any excuse and I take full responsibility . . . (The buck stops here! I'm the manager. I take the blame.)

3rd paragraph: This is what we're going to do to prevent the problem from happening again . . . (I'll show you that your letter will get action.)

4th paragraph: Meanwhile I'd like to propose . . . (reimbursement, invitation for a free visit, our sincere apology.)

5th paragraph: Don't hesitate to let me know the next time there's something wrong! By giving us your input you help us serve you better. (We want to hear from you.)

Signature,

(By the CEO)

Delta Airlines recently ran a black and white ad in the New York Times. The ad displayed 30 photos of CEOs. Each was reading a letter. Twenty-nine were smiling. The thirtieth looked stern. The text under the stern faced photo read: "I read them all and I answer them all."

Not many companies systematically encourage their customers to write to them. Fewer still supply an address. The client communication department should be able to transcribe letters and responses on word processing equipment, store them in memory, follow them up, and analyze the results. When handling complaints, it is a good policy to exceed the customer's demand. Better to reimburse $25 for a $20 demand than to lose 95 percent of the unhappy customers. Forcing the customer to enter a verbal tug-of-war can be a risky business. One runs the risk of compromising other components of the company communications program. An attractive ad campaign will be negated if a customer can't get a straight answer to questions. Give the customer a contact point! Ikea, the furniture retailer, understands. Next to each set of furniture on display, they install two small boxes and a pencil. In one, the buyer finds the order form; in the other, an evaluation form. The customer has the feeling that somebody wants his or her opinion and that they will take it seriously.

The more difficult it is for the customer to complain, the quieter dissatisfied customers will be. But, consider the 4 percent answer rate. Multiply the number of complaint letters by 100 and divide by 4. The result is a good indication of the number of customers who can be categorized "exasperated."

The Opinion of Others

A company can track the rate at which a product is returned and measure the rate of repeat business. The opinions of personnel in direct contact with the customer are a precious source of information. These people often hold the key to service solutions. Delivery, sales, and repair people, tellers and housekeeping staff all encounter happy customers and unhappy customers. They are the only ones who know why the customers feel the way they do.

Although an "image study" is generally used to assess the reputation of a firm or to measure the effectiveness of an advertising campaign, it can also cover customer satisfaction or at least measure the way in which the existing and potential customers perceive the company's promise. However, an image study tends to reveal the expectations of the market rather than the degree of satisfaction.

Finally, the number of dissatisfied customers can be assessed by counting the number of customers who have been reimbursed each year. But a reimbursed customer should not be confused with a dissatisfied customer. If the company has a very restrictive reimbursement policy, there may be more dissatisfied customers than reimbursed customers.

Putting oneself in the customer's position remains the most effective way to learn about the quality of a service. The executive might occasionally phone her own company. She can pose as a customer and ask for information. That's the fastest way to learn about service! If she wants to know if the delivery system is satisfactory, she can have something delivered to her neighbor or in-laws. The results will have no statistical value, but they can give a good idea of what the customers are receiving. Too many CEOs are content with the service supplied by their companies because they do not have to wait in line when they arrive at one of their hotels. They get immediate repair when they drive into one of the garages in their chain. They get a big smile when they walk into one of their department stores.

It is easy for facts to get obscured. In certain insurance policies, for example, the fine print mandates that to cancel the policy, a registered letter must be sent 30 days before the expiration date. If the notification is not received, the policy is automatically renewed. Although there are many insureds "in spite of themselves," contract renewals often provide the basis by which some firms calculate satisfaction. In the same way, if only 10 percent of complaints are recognized, and if only 10 percent of the complaints are indemnified, the balance sheet will show a minimum number of refunds. If the refund rate is the standard by which the firm measures satisfaction, the company will—wrongfully—be very satisfied with itself.

To summarize, the level of excellence delivered does not necessarily correspond to customer perception. To know how the customer really feels, it is necessary to ask his opinion and to pose the question in a way that makes sense to him. It is also necessary to conduct surveys that are designed to minimize contamination. The results of surveys should be compared with the competition's results when possible. Satisfaction rates must be compared with repeat business statistics. Even when a problem seems to be an exceptionally rare one, it must be taken seriously and fully investigated. Be assured: It is possible to know what the customer thinks, but sometimes it takes a bit of courage.

Self-diagnosis

- Do you perform regular surveys to measure the satisfaction of your customers?
- What is the satisfaction rate of your customers?
- What was it last year? Two years ago?
- How do your results compare with those of the competition?

- What is the rate of repeat business for your service? For satisfied customers? For dissatisfied customers?
- How many customers do you lose each year?
- How many complaint letters do you receive each year? What is the ratio between the number of complaint letters and the number of dissatisfied customers?
- How many compliment letters do you receive each year?
- How much time do you take to answer complaints?
- Do you display compliment letters?
- Do you have a clear procedure, appropriately communicated, for customers to express themselves?

―――――

CHAPTER NINE

Happy Moments, Sad Moments

W HILE writing this book I decided to keep a record of my service quality experiences. I was convinced that I would meet situations of flawless service and botched service in practically equal numbers.

As I reread the notebook in which I conscientiously set down my adventures, I discovered, to my stupefaction, that it contained mostly horror stories. Was fortune frowning on me? Was my eye particularly critical? One thing is sure; it is considerably easier to lose a customer than to win one.

It was very difficult to choose among the hundreds of stories shared by friends. I selected the ones that seemed the most instructive. I ask the companies mentioned here not to think that I am being spiteful. I would be quite happy to tell them all about the misadventures I experienced with their competitors.

O'Hare Airport

TWA is remodeling its departure desks. Half of them are closed and staffing has been reduced accordingly. To make things just perfect, three flights for New York are taking off at the same time. No need to draw pictures. Long lines form at the few open desks and my flight finally departs, 45 minutes late.

Moral: The customer must pay twice for the overhaul of the TWA desks, once by buying a ticket and a second time by missing a business appointment.

What Has Sheraton Done For You Lately?

At the Worcester, Massachusetts Sheraton, the weary traveler can order a variety of room service breakfasts every morning except Sunday. To celebrate the day of rest, management offers a Sunday breakfast buffet (in the main dining room) for $15 a head. The cost is the same if one visits the buffet five times or merely wants a bowl of cold cereal. You eat the buffet or you walk to McDonalds.

Moral: Systems designed to be provider (not customer) friendly, often leave few alternatives. That is until the next time the guest stays in Worcester.

Le Grille

Le Grille has positioned itself as a family restaurant. It offers a menu of old-style favorites (peanut butter, jelly, and banana sandwiches, for example). The restaurant is famous for its white paper table covers. Each table is topped-off with a wine glass full of crayolas. Customers, young and old alike, are invited to create masterpieces while waiting or between courses. Before any table cover is discarded, waiters are instructed to look for outstanding pieces of table art. Selected contributions are mounted and displayed as part of the decor. It's a pleasure to take the children to Le Grille.

Moral: Details overlooked by the competition can often provide a competitive edge.

National Rent-A-Car

Early one Saturday morning I called to rent a car. At the end of 30 rings, I hung up. (Maybe they're not yet open.) I try again a little later.

Finally, the operator answers and says, "I'm going to find someone to take care of you,"

I wait a good five minutes, after which I give up. Avis took good care of me.

Moral: It is not enough to have a big name and a big fleet to be successful in the car rental business.

Compeco Dry Cleaners

I stop in on my way home to pick up a trench coat which I'm having altered. (I also happen to have with me three shirts that I will need in the morning, as I have a 10 o'clock flight. If the cleaner can guarantee their delivery, I will happily have them do the job.) The woman at the counter is involved with a customer. He's a military officer who has come to pick up some uniforms that had been dry cleaned. He informs the clerk that she should keep his bill since as a long-time customer, he has an agreement with her manager to pay his dry cleaning bills once per month. The clerk contends that she never heard of the arrangement and doesn't know where to contact her boss. The officer can either pay now or leave his uniforms behind. It makes no difference to her. He stomps out the door.

Now it's my turn. I ask after my trench coat. She says that she will check on the coat after she takes my shirts. However, she can't guarantee the shirts until Thursday morning. Again, I ask about my coat.

"Another grouchy customer, huh?" she responds.

Moral: At Compeco, customers are not allowed to be grouchy. Only clerks have that privilege.

The Vet

A friend took her Siberian Husky to the veterinarian. She suspected that the dog had a fractured leg. Since it was not possible for her to leave the office early, the vet agreed to stay late in order to treat "Nikko." The leg was indeed broken. Nikko's leg was splinted and he was given a mild sedative. Friend and dog did not leave the vet's office until nearly 10:00 PM.

The next morning the doctor called to check on Nikko's condition, recommended ways to guarantee his comfort for the coming day and offered his home phone number should any further difficulties arise.

Moral: Sometimes dogs get treated better than humans.

A Mercedes Dealer

I went to a Mercedes dealer, having decided to acquire an automobile whose reputation we all know.

A salesman is talking to me, but interrupts himself each time a new customer comes in. At the end of several interruptions, I leave exasperated. Obviously, I did not buy the Mercedes.

Moral: One does not sell a service with a "good morning, sir."

Gene Walters' Market Place

A middle-sized grocery store chain in Virginia serves its busy clientele by getting back to a 1950s tradition. Call the store and dictate your grocery list. Specify brands and cuts of meat or leave it to the personal shopper. The order is delivered at your convenience. And that's not all. The delivery person is authorized to accept cash, checks, or credit cards. And they even put the groceries away for you!

Moral: One man's "old-style service" is another man's competitive edge.

Expired Inspection Sticker

I confess. I was recently stopped for driving with an expired state inspection sticker. I received a summons to appear in court at 10:00 AM on the last Thursday in September. Unfortunately, I had to be out of town the entire last week of the month, and moreover, the designated courthouse was an hour's drive from both my home and office.

I check with my insurance company to see if the violation will increase my premiums. I'm informed that my offense is a minor one and that the charge is usually dropped upon presentation of a receipt proving that the car had been inspected.

Next, I phone the court office. Yes, the offense is considered a minor one. No, I cannot have the court date changed (since the offense is *so* minor). Yes, EIS charges are usually dropped, but only at the discretion of the arresting officer. His work number should be on my warrant.

The officer is difficult to reach as he's generally on his beat. Finally, he returns my call. Yes, he would be happy to recommend that my charge be dropped. No, he will not assume responsibility for remembering our conversation. If I can find him at the courthouse, he will recommend dropping charges. (But a trip to the courthouse is what I've been trying to avoid all along.)

It's now the last Monday in September. I call the court office and explain my plight. The lady suggests that I drive to the court house and pay the fine and court costs. (Has no one been listening?) Yes, there is an alternative. I can mail the payment, but it must be processed before 10:00 AM on Thursday.

I hurry to the post office. I xerox a copy of my inspection receipt and send it with a check for the proper amount. I'm assured that Express Mail will have it delivered no later than Wednesday. Just to make sure, I also send it Express/Registered.

Two weeks later, I receive a bill from the court asking for more money. I was tried (in absentia) and found guilty. That means I owe an extra $25. What happened?

I call the court clerk. She takes 10 minutes to find the records of my case. Yes, my check was received. Yes, it is noted that the correspondence was sent Express/Registered and it arrived at 4:30 PM on Wednesday. Unfortunately, one of the clerks was getting married Thursday morning and being short-handed, the remaining staff did not post the late Wednesday mail until noon on Thursday. I was scheduled to be in court at 10:00 AM. That's why I was found guilty in my absence and fined an extra $25.

Moral: For my next book, I will consider adding "marriage of clerks" as a factor in determining service quality.

Gold and Silver Mastercards

My wife and I had separate Mastercard accounts. She used a gold card and I used a silver card. One day, while paying bills, I noticed that both payments were to be sent to an identical office. I wrote one check and noted the amounts that were to be credited to each of the accounts (including account numbers). I made a similar notation in the proper space on each of the billing slips. I enclosed the two billing slips and the check in the same envelope and sent them off.

A week later I received a phone call demanding that I make a payment on my card. I explained what I had done and was told, "You can't do that!. That's not the way the system is set up. We can't credit two accounts from the same check. That would be too complicated."

Not wishing to make life too complicated for Mastercard, I paid off both accounts and soon received a set of brand new cards from the competition.

Moral: Company-friendly (as opposed to customer-friendly) accounting systems lose customers.

Con-Ed

Most New Yorkers would prefer to spar with Mike Tyson than deal with Consolidated-Edison (the electric company).

That fact made a colleague's recent experience all the more remarkable.

She called Con-Ed to get electric service connected for an apartment she intended to lease for her business. The account executive who was assigned the call was exceptionally helpful. First, he suggested that if she listed the apartment in her own name the rates would be considerably cheaper than if she listed it as a business property. After admitting that the apartment building did not fall into his sector, he provided the name and extension number of the person who would be responsible. He asked a few more questions and suggested a few short-cuts to expediting the process. Finally, he invited my colleague "to get back to him" if anything was unnecessarily delayed.

The colleague was stunned. This from Con-Ed?

Moral: Service quality can sometimes be found where you least expect it.

The Concorde and Manhattan Taxis

I am flying to New York for a business meeting. Since I'm short on time, I spend the extra money to fly The Concorde. The Concorde is generally used by business travelers. It's not surprising to find the passenger list comprised entirely of males.

A short time before landing, passengers are presented with a toilet kit so that they may freshen up a bit. When the flight attendant reached my seat, she informed me that I would receive a set of women's toilet articles. They had run out of men's toilet kits. Run out? Men comprise over 90 percent of their business. How could they run out? I was a dissatisfied customer.

In order to reach my meeting, I flagged a New York taxi. New York cabbies have a reputation for being tough and insensitive. My driver was a pleasant surprise. He understood that I was running late and drove accordingly. When we were approaching my destination, he took care to ask which side of the avenue would be more convenient. (It was raining and he noted that de-cabbing on the wrong side of the street might incur a two-minute wait for a light change).

The cabbie received a handsome tip.

Moral: Price is not always a guarantee of service quality.

The Chernobyl Castastrophe—Cultural Differences

While no word at all from French authorities was reaching the French, all the Japanese embassies and consulates received instructions to invite Japanese citizens abroad to go to their offices for an information session to provide advice about health and food.

Moral: There are public services that actually provide service to the public.

The Hotel Frantel

Between the first course and the main course, my guest and I waited one hour. Upon departure, a very courteous head waiter asked if everything was fine. He will never know that we will never come back to his restaurant. He was trying to charm our stomachs, but we wanted fast service.

Moral: Service quality is a bottomless source of misunderstandings.

A Good Insurance Story

I had a crack in my windshield. I remember the morning when a stone from a gravel truck cracked it. The crack seemed to get longer every day.

A friend suggested that most windshield problems are covered by standard auto insurance policies.

I called the insurance company. Yes, the company would replace my windshield. I was given a number to call to make an appointment and supplied with a code number to expedite the glass company's paper work.The glass company offered me two choices: I could bring the car to them for the replacement or they would send a service truck and do the job at my home. I chose the latter. The glass man arrived punctually. He carefully scraped my state and city stickers from the old windshield. He then installed the new one, reapplied the decals and concluded his visit by washing all the windows in the car.

Moral: TARP statistics may have to be revised. I have now told hundreds of people about my pleasant experience.

The Plaza-Athenèè

After three days of questionable service from various departments of one of New York's more prestigious hotels, I took the plunge (with fingers crossed) and invited a few members of my staff to dinner in the elegant Le Regence. The maitre d' and the waiters took pains to speak French as often as possible. The menu was bilingual and featured some excellent fare.

We ordered a drink. After considerable debate, the dinner and wine orders were placed. The waiter then insisted that we order our dessert. Someone suggested that they weren't yet sure whether or not they wanted dessert. The waiter insisted: "If mademoiselle wishes dessert, we must make the order *now*".

Of course the waiter didn't know why we had to order our meal in this peculiar fashion. But because he was dealing with a table full of service quality experts, he was not allowed to escape without summoning his supervisor. The head waiter explained that the orders were necessary this early because each dessert received the personal attention of the dessert chef. He designed each dish as if it were a work of art, and, of course, he needed time to work his magic. On the assumption that there might be a shred of truth to that statement, we dutifully ordered desserts.

When they arrived, they all looked the same. They were all dressed in the same sauce and garnished with raspberries and mint leaves. For this we had to commit ourselves before we even tasted a salad?

We spent the rest of the evening trying to list possible reasons for this strange policy. In the end we unanimously agreed: The dessert chef had a heavy date. We had to order early so that he could be on time.

Moral: If someone had leveled with us, we might have understood. But as it stands, the only time any of us will return to the restaurant is on one of those days when we want to order dessert with our salad.

My Neighborhood Bookstore

A friend recently opened a bookstore. He's doing marvelously well. He says he sells books. And, yes, he does. Actually he delivers a superior service quality to people interested in books.

He makes it a point to welcome every new customer to the shop. He explains how his operation works, while taking the customer on a tour of the facility. The customer gives him vital information: name, address, phone and general and specific reading and collecting interests. He prepares bi-monthly mailings, listing titles in stock and ones due to arrive in the next 30 days. The customer is invited to order ahead. Every month he lists at least one book whose author will make an appearance at the store. If one collects autographed editions he will have one inscribed with the dedication of your choice at no extra cost. The newsletter lists the topics for the Sunday afternoon discussion sessions that the shop sponsors and occasionally includes short biographies of the people who have recently joined his Book Nut List.

On Sunday afternoons, he encourages interested people to join him for an informal discussion of some especially interesting book. (Everyone interested in the discussion has had ample time to read the book since it was listed in the newsletter.) The book seller provides refreshments.

During the holidays, he offers a special line of gift books so that book lovers can do their best to convert friends. Since gift books might mean converts, they sell at 20 percent off list. Of course gift wrapping is free.

Saturday mornings are set aside for children. Parents are invited to bring the children into the shop and read to them, or let them read to themselves, from the children's book section. Children's size chairs are provided, along with hot chocolate and apple juice for refreshments. (It always amazes me how many of those children's books find homes on Saturday morning.)

Moral: More shops like this and Guttenberg could once more become a very popular guy in my neighborhood.

NYC Public Transportation

I have to travel 10 blocks to my meeting. I'd like to take a bus. It costs $1.00 (in tokens or change). Unfortunately, I have neither.

The bus stops. I try to get on. The bus driver cannot accept a dollar bill. He tells me to go to the store on the corner and get change.

The store on the corner does *not* make change unless you buy something for over $1.00. They also stopped selling bus tokens three years ago. No profit in it.

I buy enough chewing gum to pass the $1.00 minimum and get enough change for my bus ride. As the bus pulls up to the corner it hits a puddle and splashes me (and my brief-case) with the residue of last night's rain shower.

Armed with chewing gum and a wet brief case, I arrive for my meeting.

Moral: There's a good reason why public transportation is losing ridership. Unless you're a regular and know the ropes, they don't make it easy for you to use it.

My New Chairs—December 31

I've purchased some new furniture from an up-scale retail-er. They deliver. They'll call and tell me when. Finally the call comes: My furniture will be delivered on December 31. They can't tell me what time. It's up to me to hang around. Three days before the 31st, they notify me that part of my order will not be delivered on time. I would have to wait two weeks longer for the tables but the chairs will be delivered. The long-awaited day finally arrives. I would have chairs for my New Year's Eve party!

But fortune frowns on me. At 9:00 AM, I discover that the apartment building interphone is out of order. Have the de-livery people already come and gone? Yes! I call the store to propose some possible solutions—all rejected with no appeal:

"Can you notify the delivery people?"

"Impossible. No radio in the truck."

"Can I call them at the next customer's place?"

"Impossible. Can't give out customer's addresses."

"Could you call them yourself, at the next customer's place?"

"Impossible. We can't bother our customers."

And to add to my great joy, they explain to me that the de-livery people are going to keep their truck for New Year's Eve so, according to them, my furniture might be stolen in the meantime. I ask for a new delivery date. Only the delivery manager is authorized to give a date. He's at the doctor's office and won't be back until Monday. I ask for the sales manager. He tells me that only the president has the right to order a delivery schedule shorter than the regular one. Bad luck again, he has gone off skiing.

In desperation, I rent a truck and pick up the furniture at the warehouse.

Do I have to tell you how long it was until the tables were finally delivered? Of course, there was no sign of a letter of apology for either situation.

Moral: The furniture business must be in pretty good shape.

Enough! I believe I've made my point. Since my story notebook is full, maybe one day I'll write another book: a bible about sure ways to lose (or win) customers. As you have seen, there are no shortage of ways.

Self-diagnosis

- Prepare your own "blunder book" for one month, noting all the happy and sad moments in your daily life.
- Ask the people who use your services to do the same thing.
- What are the lessons that you draw from your company?
- A new opening or opportunity? A new segment to attack?
- Improve your standards? Your service delivery system?
- Improve your error chase?

CHAPTER TEN

How to Launch a
Service Quality Program

BY NOW, you know that the customer always wants better service quality. You also know that the customer's conception of quality is not necessarily the same as yours. You've already decided to compete with a policy of service quality rather than declare a price war. How do you start a service quality program in your company? You know that there's room for improvement. But you have a lot of questions:

- Does the quality promise match market expectations?
- Is the quality promise clearly formulated? Is it usable from the top to the bottom of the organization?
- Is the promise competitive? Is it adequately communicated to potential customers?
- Are there quality standards? If so, are they measurable? Are they known to everyone in the company? Does the service delivered conform to the standards?
- Does the service match the identified level of excellence?
- Is it in the implementation stage that the quality slips?
- Is the customer content? What else can be done for the customer to maintain a competitive advantage?

To answer these questions, there is only one thing to do: Ask the customer! Conduct a survey. Use interviews and questionnaires. This will enable you to continually monitor all the people upon whom the success of your company depends.

Find out what your customers want. What are their needs? How can they be served? What is the competition doing? If there are no similar products, look at what is being done in analogous sectors. If you want to design a computer repair service procedure, look at what appliance or typewriter repair people are doing. Above all, don't forget the employees who are in direct contact with the customers. They know plenty!

What you learn from the customer will enable you to diagnose the health of your service. The resultant diagnosis should specify whether you must completely rethink your quality policy or whether you must improve it with some fine-tuning.

Diagnosis, The Inevitable Starting Point

Is the service quality problem the accumulation of errors all along the chain? Is the service promise always kept? Is quality too much in the hands of the front-line supervisor, the store manager, the delivery or repair people? Does quality vary from one location to another? How? Is the competition catching up? How? All of these questions are part of a proper service quality diagnosis.

Putting too much faith in the instruments used in the diagnosis can also be a mistake. Most banks do not directly survey customer satisfaction. They merely track the number of accounts closed and the degree of activity in the remaining accounts. These two performance indicators will never tell them why an account has been closed or become inactive.

Diagnosis is the keystone of any quality program. It will tell the manager whether he or she must initiate an error chase to try for zero defect or give the quality strategy a complete review.

A diagnosis is always more difficult for the market leader. The leader often prefers to rest on its laurels. Thanks to lack of vigilance, the quality of its service slowly deteriorates. It takes courage to react and accept change. The market leader needs more alarm signals than others, because there is always a lag between service shortcomings and falling sales. And the leader's self-image plays against it. It can mask faults.

The customer may be more lenient, assuming that the leader knows best. (After all, that's why it's the leader.) That is, until the day the customer switches to the competition. To the leader's dismay, the customer may have discovered a better, less expensive alternative.

The number one position, in itself, may be a handicap. Many customers are suspicious of the leader, prejudging the leader's arrogance and preferring to do business with someone who may be more appreciative. The Japanese have used this behavior to their advantage. Penetrating markets from the bottom, they surround their products with superior service. They nibble away at local competitors and finally take over the market with a superior product and service quality. The day when they will be able to dominate insurance, banking, and chain retailing is on the way. In less than a decade, Japanese banks have become the world's largest.

Self-diagnosis is always difficult when everything is going well. After all, "Where's the beef?" How does the restaurant manager motivate the staff to do better when the place is always packed? Why work harder when all the tables are occupied, when crowds are being turned away and when the restaurant is doing well even during August?

To know whether a diagnosis is valid, it may be necessary to ask whether it answers three questions: Is the quality level good? Is the quality level respected? Finally, is it better than the competition?

In Quest of Zero Defect

Small quality errors are the most difficult to track down. They are generally far from the home office on the customer's premises, in the various stores of a chain, or in other countries. They might also be happening 24 hours a day. Some aspects of a service are better than the competition. In others, the competition may have the lead. Eliminating these small service errors is the responsibility of everyone in the organization. Maintaining the level of excellence everywhere and at all times is a fundamental job. In fact, it must become an obsession. It's not enough to create a service quality control department.

Quality circles and the participation of staff in direct contact with the customers will be particularly effective. Every initiative will help in avoiding or correcting errors, hence to perfecting the quality structure. The error chase must be an all-consuming discipline. It's not just a question of method.

Employees must be taught to be proud to do it right the first time. Little victories must be rewarded. Quality circles must meet often and regularly. On average, a quality circle will produce about 20 perceptible improvements. These little improvements will directly influence the customer's judgment.

All the quality champions apply the same rule; it is better to try to improve 100 details by 1 percent than to try for 100 percent progress on a single aspect of service. Only systematic effort produces tangible results. A quest for zero defect can't be improvised. Here are the main steps:

- Make sure that the quality standards are shared by everyone. (It is useless to ask someone to do it right the first time if she does not know exactly what to do.)

- Standards must be clear and specific.
- They must also match your promise. (Sometimes they have to be respecified for the various parts of the organization.)
- They must be understood by all the people concerned. (A service company employing 10,000 people, must create from 1,000 to 3,000 standards, dependent upon the complexity of the service.)
- Assess the work to be accomplished and the time it will take to communicate clear standards to the employees.

Define the Priorities

The error chase must not run off in all directions. It is essential that the chase be conducted with clearly stated priorities. What comes first? The welcome? Response speed? Service time? Complaint handling? Cleanliness? The diagnosis should provide an order of priorities. Another approach is to attack the pressing problems first and to plan more comprehensively after the brush fires have been extinguished.

This approach may not be suitable for companies having little or no familiarity with the philosophy of total quality. If the error chase is limited to only a single department, major successes will be difficult to achieve. Companies adopting the error chase for the first time need to launch a generalized campaign, beginning with the CEO.

Launching a Zero Defect Campaign for All Levels of Personnel

Once priorities are established, it is necessary to mobilize enthusiasm. A company-wide gathering will get everyone on the bandwagon. This is a first step. But it's indispensable to altering the company culture and to orienting everyone toward the customer.

The decision to strive for zero defect does not guarantee success. A company-wide communication effort will be necessary. Speeches, posters, emblems, audiovisuals, diplomas, badges, prizes, contests, logos, and slogans can each play a role. Everything must be carefully organized. No half measures. And remember, it is very difficult to attain zero defect. Perfection is not of this world!

Training for the Chase for Zero Defect

The success of an error chase depends on two factors: knowledge of the quality standards and the ability of the groups to work together. Teams must be trained to deal with both points. Seminars with the correct mix of information and discussion must be planned at regular intervals. The entire organization must be represented. It is preferable to hold the seminars within the firm rather than to send people outside. There is not a lot of literature on the subject. Most of the available documentation concerns product quality. Furthermore, "home-made" workshops and seminars symbolize top management's commitment to improve service quality, and data specific to the company will be available.

Setting Up An Error Chase Procedure

The error chase procedure is organized around two mechanisms: the establishment of the work group, and the information feedback that will be implemented. The sooner employees can observe the tangible effects of the error chase, the more they will be motivated to continue the work.

Firms that have continual contact with the customer should be certain to integrate the customer into the process. Hotels, department stores, restaurants, transportation facilities, hospitals, schools, banks, telecommunications companies, sports, and leisure activities are all areas in which the presence of the client in the working groups is indispensable.

*Measure the Progress Accomplished
and Spread the Word*

It is necessary to measure the effects of the proposed actions with regard to the clientele and to communicate the results throughout the organization as soon as possible. For this purpose, the bulletin board and the newsletter are indispensable. Don't forget to mention all the little victories in official speeches.

Bringing the Service Rendered Into Question

The quality diagnosis may conclude that there is a mismatch between the service rendered and the customer's expectations. This should come as no surprise. In this case, the work is mainly to track down errors rather than to bring the service promise into question. Quality circles won't work. Only a thorough rethinking by general management can restructure a quality strategy. It can be done!

Club Med recently realized that the expectations of German, Italian, and British vacationers were not the same as those of the French, who constituted its traditional market. First, the Club tried to satisfy everybody with a series of minor adjustments in the villages. Result: No one was satisfied.

The CEO at the time, Serge Trigano, saw two possibilities: design a new product, the international village, or arrange the villages by nationality and promote them in the appropriate countries.

He chose the first approach. Seventeen villages were selected. They were taken out of the brochure aimed at the French market, and promoted separately to Europeans. In these villages, the welcome and reception were rethought to take into account the full range of arrivals and departures. The buffet table added a variety of dishes including specialties from various European countries. The GOs were asked to speak several languages. Very quickly, the satisfaction index of the Germans, Italians, Belgians, and British rose 20 percent.

The error chase is conducted from the bottom to the top of an organization. Restructuring of the service strategy must come from the top. Employees in direct contact with the customer can signal behavior that indicates dissatisfaction, but they cannot redesign strategies. They do not possess an overall view, nor do they have the data necessary to make broad policy decisions. General management must decide whether it will be preferable to try out a new strategy on a pilot site or to implement it throughout the company. Since front-line people have the best opportunity to observe customer reactions, it is always wise to include them in the decision making.

Employee communications must be written with considerable care. It is more difficult to get a radically new, management-proposed approach accepted than it is to spread the results of a zero defect chase.

Serge Trigano brought together all the GOs of his Europe/Africa sector, in groups of 50, when he unveiled his new service strategy. A welcome book was distributed to new, nonFrench GOs to familiarize them with Club Med culture. The participants were soon sold on the new strategy.

The campaign clearly demonstrated the importance that management attached to the new villages. Nevertheless, it made sure that sales people would not designate these new villages as "purgatories," advising the French against them. It positioned them as "unique occasions" to get out of the French shell.

There are barometers that suggest that a service needs retooling. The best sign is a steady drop in the customer satisfaction rate. One must be doubly suspect when, after having rectified a number of service elements, the rate continues to drop. The competition must also be constantly monitored.

Any drop in market share means that customers are going elsewhere. Finally, no satisfaction rating (even 98 percent) is secure if the competition's rate is getting closer. One's competitive advantage may be slipping!

At the beginning of the 1980s, Singapore Airlines found itself in such a situation. Cathay Pacific was the competition. Until then, Singapore Airlines, according to its own surveys and those of international aviation, was number one in its region. Cathay Pacific began by imitating Air Singapore. Gradually, it innovated, nibbling away at the market share.

Complaint letters sent to Singapore Airlines dealt with little things. Passengers were not happy with baggage services (usually at airports where baggage handling was subcontracted) or noted that crew enthusiasm seemed to be slipping. (The drop in enthusiasm may have been the result of frequent personnel transfers.)

Singapore Airlines had two options. It could address the questions raised by the passengers or step back and reexamine its total service program. The first path would merely mean improving baggage control and stimulating a fresh team spirit among flight personnel. The second path would mean inventing new services to counter Cathay Pacific. Singapore Airlines introduced seats that were convertible for sleeping. (This strategy was later abandoned as a result of a customer survey.) Then it began offering games and a wider choice of films.

Such decisions modify each service chain. By redefining the service strategy, one modifies promises and quality standards. At the same time, it may become necessary to retrain employees, if not replace them. A new advertising campaign may also be necessary.

When Xerox entered the office automation systems business, it set up a new service chain. They could not use photocopy machine sales and repair people to serve microcomputer customers. From the operational management to information policy, everything was designed to respond to the new activity, including the customer satisfaction indicators.

A Shared Trunk of Excellence
for Several Service Branches

A company frequently serves several market segments. For each of them, it will need an appropriate quality policy plus a program for chasing errors or reevaluating total service delivery. A travel agency, for example, can address itself to tourists and to business travelers. Two different emphases, two different sets of needs, two different quality policies. However, the agency can only succeed in both markets by developing a shared trunk of excellence upon which the service branches are grafted. It will also need a homogeneous policy of high quality for welcome, telephone answering, office decoration, and staff know-how.

Another example is the auto parts dealer who serves several customer market segments. It may serve a small repair garage that can only stock a minimum parts inventory and needs frequent deliveries. It may also serve a large garage that wants efficient invoicing, inventory counseling, and volume pricing. A third customer may be a delivery firm that manages its own truck fleet and often needs maintenance assistance or repair service. Although each segment benefits from a specific service, it must also be linked to the others by a shared trunk that will provide perfect quality conformity. At IBM France, a total service quality policy dominates all the segments. It is organized around four concepts:

- a quality definition, shared by all
- preventive maintenance planning (favored mode of action)

- quality measurement, generalized throughout the company
- zero defect

Total quality management is founded on three management principles:

- top management commitment
- employee commitment (with priority given to teamwork)
- a rational approach to improving quality

A quality committee, chaired by the CEO of IBM France, meets once a month. Quality plans are integrated in the strategic planning. Performance evaluation takes into account the results achieved by quality actions. Quality circles and progress groups exist on a permanent basis. All client relations are codified with accurate measurement of deviations. Once a compliance deviation appears, an error chase is launched. From 1982 to 1985, the number of working groups, which met for approximately one hour per week, grew from 230 to approximately 900.

Conclusion

As a conclusion, I am sure you will not be surprised if I ask you to participate in a satisfaction survey. Naturally, I gathered together a number of readers in order to learn what questions to ask. They also helped me measure the quality perceived by the reader, and the quality imagined by the author. So I shall not ask you if you like the form or the sequencing logic. The qualitative survey reveals that you couldn't care less. In spite of everything, if certain questions seem valueless to you, don't hesitate to check the block labelled "stupid question." Satisfaction cannot be measured on a large scale unless it is simple for the customer to respond. The questionnaire on page 143 is to be sent to the address shown at the top of the page.

Thank you in advance for your cooperation, dear customer/reader and perhaps "see you soon" if this book satisfies you.

Please complete the following questionnaire and send responses to:
J. Horovitz
c/o Productivity Press
P.O. Box 3007
Cambridge, MA 02140

	Yes	No	Stupid question
Are you generally satisfied with this book?			
Does it keep its title's promise?			
Does it match the promise of its advertising?			
Because of This Book:			
Have you been able to perform a diagnosis of your firm's service quality?			
Have you determined three action priorities for service quality for the next year?			
Has there been some fundamental change in your way of thinking about your quality?			
Have you solved—on paper anyway—at least one service quality problem that you could not solve before?			
Do you feel that you have acquired a clear and accurate method for approaching service quality in your company?			

How many extra customers do you think you will gain thanks to this approach? _____

How many customers do you think you will keep thanks to this approach? _____

In your opinion, what chapter(s) deserved to be developed further? _____

In your opinion, what chapter(s) is (are) too long? _____

What chapter(s) do you find to be useless? _____

THANK YOU FOR YOUR HELP!

So that I can know you a bit better, could I also have the following information?

• What's your firm's primary function? _____

• Number of employees in your company? 0-49 50-99 100-499 500-999 1000-1999 2000+

• Your position? CEO/President   Middle management   Supervisor   Customer contact
                                                                                personnel

• Your department? Administration   Marketing   Sales   After-sales   Financial   Other
                                                          service

THANK YOU AGAIN!

Also from
Productivity Press

Productivity Press publishes and distributes materials on continuous improvement in productivity, quality, customer service, and the creative involvement of all employees. Many of our products are direct source materials from Japan that have been translated into English for the first time and are available exclusively from Productivity. Supplemental products and services include newsletters, conferences, seminars, in-house training and consulting, audio-visual training programs, and industrial study missions. Call 1-800-274-9911 for our free book catalog.

Championship Management
by James A. Belohlav

Many current books extol the values of being an excellent company. This book goes beyond that to explain how excellence can be achieved and why it is so critically important. A model for action explains how any company can become a "championship" caliber company. Further, it explains why some excellent companies lose their edge while others remain excellent, and why still others appear to be excellent but are not.
ISBN 0-915299-76-3 / 176 pages / $29.95 / Order code CHAMPS-BK

The Service Era
Leadership in a Global Environment
by Franco D'Egidio

Through anecdotes, case studies, and the presentation of a clear and straightforward business philosophy, this book examines the crisis of current Western business strategy in its lack of a service-oriented perspective. D'Egidio challenges management to develop both strategy and corporate culture based on the critical "moment of truth" for any business: the point of contact with the customer. After supporting the claim that quality service is more important than quality products, the book offers eight strategic directions for dealing with the challenge of competition based on a global service orientation.
ISBN 0-915299-68-2 / 96 pages / $29.95 / Order code GSM-BK

The Idea Book
Improvement Through Total Employee Involvement
edited by the Japan Human Relations Association

What would your company be like if each employee — from line workers to engineers to sales people — gave 100 ideas every year for improving the company? This handbook of Japanese-style suggestion systems (called "teian"), will help your company develop its own vital improvement system by getting all employees involved. Train workers how to write improvement proposals, help supervisors promote participation, and put creative problem solving to work in your company. Designed as a self-trainer and study group tool, the book is heavily illustrated and includes hundreds of examples. (Spanish edition available.)
ISBN 0-915299-22-4 / 232 pages / $49.95 / Order code IDEA-BK

Quality Service Idea Book
Improvements for Office and Retail Through TEI
edited by the Japan Human Relations Association

This book presents an improvement proposal system in a context designed for customer service and administrative employees. Initial chapters about why suggestions are important and how to write persuasive improvement proposals are followed by two chapters of illustrated examples and case histories from various services industries and office or administrative situations. This is a creative book that should stimulate many ideas of your own. It is a companion to our best selling *The Idea Book: Improvement through TEI.*
ISBN 0-915299-65-8 / 272 pages / $49.95 / Order code CSIDEA-BK

The Best of TEI
Current Perspectives on Total Employee Involvement
edited by Karen Jones

An outstanding compilation of the 29 best presentations from the first three International Total Employee Involvement (TEI) conferences sponsored by Productivity. You'll find sections on management strategy, case studies, training and retraining, kaizen (continuous improvement), and high quality teamwork. Here's the cutting edge in implemented EI strategies — doubly valuable to you because it comprises both theory and practice. It's also amply illustrated with presentation charts. Whether you're a manager, a team member, or in HR development, you'll find The Best of TEI a rich and stimulating source of information. Comes in handy 3-ring binder.
ISBN 0-915299-63-1 / 502 pages / $175.00 / Order code TEI-BK

Better Makes Us Best
by John Psarouthakis

A short, engaging, but powerful and highly practical guide to performance improvement for any business or individual. Focusing on incremental progress toward clear goals is the key — you become "better" day by day. It's a realistic, personally fulfilling, action-oriented, and dynamic philosophy that has made Psarouthakis's own company a member of the Fortune 500 in just ten years. Buy a copy for everyone in your work force, and let it work for you.
ISBN 0-915299-56-9 / 112 pages / $16.95 / order code BMUB-BK

The Quality and Productivity Equation
American Corporate Strategies for the 1990s
edited by Ross E. Robson

How well will your business succeed in the next decade? What challenges are in store, and how are you planning to meet them? Here's what over thirty of America's most forward-thinking business and academic leaders (including John Diebold, Malcolm Forbes, Donald Ephlin, Alan Magazine, and Wickham Skinner) are already thinking about and doing. Based on presentations made at Utah State University's College of Business "Partners in Business" seminars for 1989. Take advantage of their expertise to shape your own strategy.
ISBN 0-915299-71-2 / 558 pages / $29.95 / Order code QPE-BK

The Improvement Book
Creating the Problem-Free Workplace
by Tomo Sugiyama

A practical guide to setting up a participatory problem-solving system in the workplace. Focusing on ways to eliminate the "Big 3" problems — "irrationality, inconsistency, and waste — this book provides clear direction for starting a "problem-free engineering" program. It also gives you a full introduction to basic concepts of industrial housekeeping (known in Japan as 5S), two chapters of examples that can be used in small group training activities, and a workbook for individual use (extra copies are available separately). Written in an informal style, and using many anecdotes and examples, this book provides a proven approach to problem solving for any industrial setting.
ISBN 0-915299-47-X / 236 pages / $49.95 / Order code IB-BK

Service Insider Newsletter

The monthly Service Insider Newsletter gives you the quickest and most efficient line on the service strategies that are working and the ones that aren't. You'll gain this valuable knowledge through news stories, interviews, case studies, and quick tips. The Service Insider is written to help you be responsive to the customers of the 1990s, to keep you ahead of your competition. It brings you the information you need about how to keep your customer satisfied. To sign up, or for more information, call 1-800-888-6485. Please state code "BA" when ordering.

COMPLETE LIST OF TITLES FROM PRODUCTIVITY PRESS

Asaka, Tetsuichi and Kazuo Ozeki (eds.). **Handbook of Quality Tools: The Japanese Approach**
ISBN 0-915299-45-3 / 1990 / 325 pages / $59.95 / order code HQT

Buehler, Vernon M. and Y.K. Shetty (eds.). **Competing Through Productivity and Quality**
ISBN 0-915299-43-7 / 1989 / 576 pages / $39.95 / order code COMP

Christopher, William F. **Productivity Measurement Handbook**
ISBN 0-915299-05-4 / 1985 / 680 pages / $137.95 / order code PMH

Ford, Henry. **Today and Tomorrow**
ISBN 0-915299-36-4 / 1988 / 286 pages / $24.95 / order code FORD

Fukuda, Ryuji. **CEDAC: A Tool for Continuous Systematic Improvement**
ISBN 0-915299-26-7 / 1990 / 144 pages / $49.95 / order code CEDAC

Fukuda, Ryuji. **Managerial Engineering: Techniques for Improving Quality and Productivity in the Workplace**
ISBN 0-915299-09-7 / 1984 / 206 pages / $34.95 / order code ME

Hatakeyama, Yoshio. **Manager Revolution! A Guide to Survival in Today's Changing Workplace**
ISBN 0-915299-10-0 / 1985 / 208 pages / $24.95 / order code MREV

Hirano, Hiroyuki. **JIT Factory Revolution: A Pictorial Guide to Factory Design of the Future**
ISBN 0-915299-44-5 / 1989 / 227 pages / $49.95 / order code JITFAC

Japan Human Relations Association (ed.). **The Idea Book: Improvement Through TEI (Total Employee Involvement)**
ISBN 0-915299-22-4 / 1988 / 232 pages / $49.95 / order code IDEA

Japan Management Association (ed.). **Kanban and Just-In-Time at Toyota: Management Begins at the Workplace** (Revised Ed.), Translated by David J. Lu
ISBN 0-915299-48-8 / 1989 / 224 pages / $36.50 / order code KAN

Japan Management Association and Constance E. Dyer. **The Canon Production System: Creative Involvement of the Total Workforce**
ISBN 0-915299-06-2 / 1987 / 251 pages / $36.95 / order code CAN

Jones, Karen (ed.). **The Best of TEI: Current Perspectives on Total Employee Involvement**
ISBN 0-915299-63-1 / 1989 / 502 pages / $175.00 / order code TEI

Karatsu, Hajime. **Tough Words For American Industry**
ISBN 0-915299-25-9 / 1988 / 178 pages / $24.95 / order code TOUGH

Karatsu, Hajime. **TQC Wisdom of Japan: Managing for Total Quality Control,** Translated by David J. Lu
ISBN 0-915299-18-6 / 1988 / 136 pages / $34.95 / order code WISD

Lu, David J. **Inside Corporate Japan: The Art of Fumble-Free Management**
ISBN 0-915299-16-X / 1987 / 278 pages / $24.95 / order code ICJ

Mizuno, Shigeru (ed.). **Management for Quality Improvement: The 7 New QC Tools**
ISBN 0-915299-29-1 / 1988 / 324 pages / $59.95 / order code 7QC

Monden, Yashuhiro and Michiharu Sakurai (eds.). **Japanese Management Accounting: A World Class Approach to Profit Management**
ISBN 0-915299-50-X / 1989 / 584 pages / $59.95 / order code JMACT

Nakajima, Seiichi. **Introduction to TPM: Total Productive Maintenance**
ISBN 0-915299-23-2 / 1988 / 149 pages / $39.95 / order code ITPM

Nakajima, Seiichi. **TPM Development Program: Implementing Total Productive Maintenance**
ISBN 0-915299-37-2 / 1989 / 428 pages / $85.00 / order code DTPM

Nikkan Kogyo Shimbun, Ltd./Factory Magazine (ed.). **Poka-yoke: Improving Product Quality by Preventing Defects**
ISBN 0-915299-31-3 / 1989 / 288 pages / $59.95 / order code IPOKA

Ohno, Taiichi. **Toyota Production System: Beyond Large-Scale Production**
ISBN 0-915299-14-3 / 1988 / 162 pages / $39.95 / order code OTPS

Ohno, Taiichi. **Workplace Management**
ISBN 0-915299-19-4 / 1988 / 165 pages / $34.95 / order code WPM

Ohno, Taiichi and Setsuo Mito. **Just-In-Time for Today and Tomorrow**
ISBN 0-915299-20-8 / 1988 / 165 pages / $34.95 / order code OMJIT

Psarouthakis, John. **Better Makes Us Best**
ISBN 0-915299-56-9 / 1989 / 112 pages / $16.95 / order code BMUB

Robson, Ross (ed.). **The Quality and Productivity Equation: American Corporate Strategies for the 1990s**
ISBN 0-915299-71-2 / 1990 / 558 pages / $29.95 / order code QPE

Shingo, Shigeo. **Non-Stock Production: The Shingo System for Continuous Improvement**
ISBN 0-915299-30-5 / 1988 / 480 pages / $75.00 / order code NON

Shingo, Shigeo. **A Revolution In Manufacturing: The SMED System,** Translated by Andrew P. Dillon
ISBN 0-915299-03-8 / 1985 / 383 pages / $70.00 / order code SMED

Shingo, Shigeo. **The Sayings of Shigeo Shingo: Key Strategies for Plant Improvement,** Translated by Andrew P. Dillon
ISBN 0-915299-15-1 / 1987 / 208 pages / $39.95 / order code SAY

Shingo, Shigeo. **A Study of the Toyota Production System from an Industrial Engineering Viewpoint** (Revised Ed.),
ISBN 0-915299-17-8 / 1989 / 293 pages / $39.95 / order code STREV

Shingo, Shigeo. **Zero Quality Control: Source Inspection and the Poka-yoke System,** Translated by Andrew P. Dillon
ISBN 0-915299-07-0 / 1986 / 328 pages / $70.00 / order code ZQC

Shinohara, Isao (ed.). **New Production System: JIT Crossing Industry Boundaries**
ISBN 0-915299-21-6 / 1988 / 224 pages / $34.95 / order code NPS

Sugiyama, Tomo. **The Improvement Book: Creating the Problem-free Workplace**
ISBN 0-915299-47-X / 1989 / 236 pages / $49.95 / order code IB

Suzue, Toshio and Akira Kohdate. **Variety Reduction Program (VRP): A Production Strategy for Product Diversification**
ISBN 0-915299-32-1 / 1990 / 164 pages / $59.95 / order code VRP

Tateisi, Kazuma. **The Eternal Venture Spirit: An Executive's Practical Philosophy**
ISBN 0-915299-55-0 / 1989 / 208 pages / $19.95 / order code EVS

AUDIO-VISUAL PROGRAMS

Japan Management Association. **Total Productive Maintenance: Maximizing Productivity and Quality**
ISBN 0-915299-46-1 / 167 slides / 1989 / $749.00 / order code STPM
ISBN 0-915299-49-6 / 2 videos / 1989 / $749.00 / order code VTPM

Shingo, Shigeo. **The SMED System**, Translated by Andrew P. Dillon
ISBN 0-915299-11-9 / 181 slides / 1986 / $749.00 / order code S5
ISBN 0-915299-27-5 / 2 videos / 1987 / $749.00 / order code V5

Shingo, Shigeo. **The Poka-yoke System**, Translated by Andrew P. Dillon
ISBN 0-915299-13-5 / 235 slides / 1987 / $749.00 / order code S6
ISBN 0-915299-28-3 / 2 videos / 1987 / $749.00 / order code V6

TO ORDER: Write, phone, or fax Productivity Press, Dept. BK, P.O. Box 3007, Cambridge, MA 02140, phone 1-800-274-9911, fax 617-868-3524. Send check or charge to your credit card (American Express, Visa, MasterCard accepted).

U.S. ORDERS: Add $4 shipping for first book, $2 each additional. CT residents add 8% and MA residents 5% sales tax.

FOREIGN ORDERS: Payment must be made in U.S. dollars (checks must be drawn on U.S. banks). For Canadian orders, add $10 shipping for first book, $2 each additional. For orders to other countries write, phone, or fax for quote and indicate shipping method desired.

NOTE: Prices subject to change without notice.